guiding the

reader to

the next

book

Edited by
KENNETH D. SHEARER

 Neal-Schuman Publishers, Inc.
New York   London

Published by Neal-Schuman Publishers, Inc.
100 Varick Street
New York, NY 10013

Printed and bound in the United States America

Library of Congress Cataloging-in-Publication Data

Shearer, Kenneth D.
    Guiding the reader to the next book / by Kenneth Shearer.
        p.   cm.
    Includes bibliographical references (p.) and index.
    ISBN 1-55570-209-0 (alk. paper)
    1. Reader guidance—United States.   2. Fiction in libraries.
I. Title.
Z711.4.S53   1996
025.5'4—dc20

                                                          96-7255
                                                          CIP

Contents

Preface

$\mathcal{F}$inding the proverbial "needle in the haystack" is what library service is all about. The ability to find the particular fact, phrase, or work of fiction that perfectly meets the needs of an individual from among the avalanche of available (some less than perfect) alternatives, is a distinguishing attribute of most memorable library professionals.

Libraries not only locate needed information, they also recommend good reading. Books expand the imagination, knowledge, spirit, understanding, ideas, and social world of their users. On occasion, the readers' advisor's guidance leads a patron to stories which compellingly speak to her and help her in her own life. Much more often, advice leads to reading that is somewhat helpful. Unfortunately, other reading advice is completely off base and not worth pursuing. *Guiding the Reader to the Next Book* works to make that occasional experience occur more frequently. Each chapter in this book covers an important area of readers' advisory service, as illustrated below.

Chapter One, by Kenneth Shearer, covers not only what is needed for a good readers' advisory transaction, but also offers examples of successful and unsuccessful transactions. Because searching for leisure reading is the most common use of public libraries, library staff must be able to give advice on what to do next, and library marketing efforts must stress that libraries offer this valuable advice. This chapter offers a rare description of how readers' advisory transactions actually take place.

Chapter Two, by Pauletta Brown Bracy, goes the next step by offering case studies and suggestions for a specific reader audience. In this chapter, the attention shifts to readers' advisory service regarding materials for children and young adults. It also deals with children's and young adult literature—an area in which professional education places more emphasis on reader guidance—and as well offers additional insights in the effectiveness of reader guidance in practice.

Chapter Three, by Duncan Smith, explores a librarian's point of view of what books mean to readers. To serve clients well, librarians need to reflect on the role that reading plays in the very private inner monologue of the reader. It is only there that the value and meaning of readers' advisory service can be realized fully. We should evaluate our own experiences with reading, but we must also recognize that others have different reactions to books and readers. This chapter is unique because it explores one actual reader's experience in choosing materials with the help of the librarian.

Chapter Four, by Robert Burgin, examines current readers' advisory practices. Who actually provides advice to readers in public libraries today? How well-prepared are they? How well-read are they? A survey of how the readers' advisor does her job is included here and raises questions about their preparation for—and continuing education in—readers' advisory service.

Chapter Five, also by Duncan Smith, reports on an experiment allowing readers' advisors to check on how well-aimed their recommendations are. The advisee in this experiment was able to provide feedback to the advisor about his or recommendation, creating a fascinating feedback loop. The reader can check his or her own score in predicting what a reader would like to read next and see firsthand why skillful probing is essential.

Chapter Six is written by Sharon Baker, a frequent contributor to the literature on the "browsability" of fiction collections. The author filters through the considerable research in this area and relates the major implications for practice. Understanding how readers "browse" and ultimately choose fiction is a key to becoming a successful readers' advisor.

Chapter Seven, by Gail Harrell, examines the use of fiction categories in major public libraries. Virtually all nonfiction collections in public libraries in the United States are classified according to the Dewey Decimal system; organization of fiction collections is far less standardized, however. This survey of fiction classes in use in American libraries shows that a few genres are common, especially in adult collections, but major work remains to be done in this area.

Chapter Eight, by Jeffrey Cannell and Eileen McCluskey, discusses the issue of classification and its effect on circulation. What impact, if any, does the classification of novels according to major genres have on the use of fiction in public libraries? An experiment reported in this chapter shows clearly that the payoff is immediate and dramatic.

Chapter Nine, also by Kenneth Shearer, reviews that the findings in this book, along with attendant developments in readers' advisory tools, strongly suggest that readers' advisory practice is changing.

Two appendixes give additional information. Appendix A offers a wealth of readers' advisory sources on the Internet. The Internet can be a source of both information and solace to the readers' advisor. Groups share tidbits of information on all the major fiction genres. There are also Web sites where the advisor can pose those tough-to-answer inquires. Appendix B provides an annotated bibliography of fiction classification. The unresolved, but very important issue of how to classify fiction in public libraries (i.e. how to make manageable recreational readers' searches for likely-to-please them novels) has generated a considerable amount of literature over time. This annotated bibliography eases the task of grasping what the literature has to offer in this area.

Understanding reader's advisory services, regardless of your role in the library, will help you to understand your patrons better. I was once the patron in the library, and it was my readers' advisor who had a profound effect on me. Her name was Marion Humble, she was a public librarian, and she was one of my most influential teachers during high school. A good listener, she employed her formidable intellect, fine taste, and wide-ranging knowledge in the task of suggesting books which were well-written, challenging, and memorable. She epitomized what I later learned was called the readers' advisor (an idea developed in the 1920s and 1930s)—a librarian who helped match readers and books. Her work profoundly altered my life. I am grateful for her influence. Later, while I was pursuing my MLS degree, I learned this skill in part by acquaintance with a stunning array of reference works, bibliographies, indexes, and abstracting services. It was then that I realized that a good readers' advisor is a treasure—any term paper or doctoral dissertation could be vastly improved with the help of a professional readers' advisor.

Of course librarians are not the only source of suggested reading. Book reviews, bookstore staff, authors' suggestions in the books we read, teachers, friends, talk programs, and acquaintances all may contribute to our enjoyment of and benefit from reading. Not all readers, furthermore, are always open to the ways of Marion Humble. Indeed, only in certain formative times of life—times which will differ from one individual to another and which are most likely to be opportunities seen by children's and young adult librarians—can reading advice make such a major difference for an individual. This book addresses these librarians' efforts to guide readers. Areas such as separating mysteries from other fiction books, providing new books in attractive displays, offering individualized consultation services, programs featuring writers, and preparing customized local readers' advisory tools as well as shelved books from which to choose are all ways of providing a wealth of readers' advisory services. After reading *Guiding the Reader to the Next Book,* we hope you will use the suggestions and reach out to your patrons as an informed and effective readers' advisor.

Part I:
Readers' Advisory Services:
The State of the Art

Chapter One:
The Nature of the Readers' Advisory Transaction in Adult Reading

by Kenneth Shearer

*I*n an article entitled "Readers' Advisory Services: A Call for More Research," Sharon Baker points out that the first surge of readers' advisory work—during the 1920s and 1930s—failed to evolve because its value had not been demonstrated to library managers who were forced to cut back operations during the Depression. There was no research that established why, during a budgetary crunch, readers' advisory service ought to be prioritized. She writes that "...there is almost no research on the extent to which direct help from a readers' advisor can increase patron satisfaction with or use of library resources."[1]

Baker observes that this issue

> . . . is of particular concern, since parallel research has shown that patrons receive more accurate answers to their reference questions and have higher satisfaction rates if the reference librarian successfully asks a series of factual questions to help uncover the patron's real information need.[1]

Shearer and Bracy have responded to Baker's article. Their preliminary findings are reported fully in this book.[2]

This and the following chapter report on baseline research in readers' advisory service, thus helping to form the foundation that

Baker seeks. This exploratory research concerns the nature of the transaction that takes place in a public library when a user asks for reading advice. This may, in fact, be the initial study of readers' advisory transactions as they actually take place.

Research on the reference transaction in library settings, especially Durrance's assessment of reference service delivery, is influential in shaping this work. Durrance's students visit libraries with reference questions and report on a variety of concerns about reference service success: the placement of reference areas in the library, use of related signage, the reference transaction, and whether the student surrogate clients would return for more help, a very useful "bottom line" manner of assessing the value of a "free" library service.[3]

Durrance shared a copy of the instrument she was using with this investigator. It was used one summer session in an introductory survey course and found to be a very good device to sensitize students to the user side of the reference desk. That experience, combined with an interest in readers' advisory transactions, led this investigator to completely revise Durrance's instrument in order to explore the questions set forth here. The debt to Durrance is great.

Recently, Dewdney and Ross wrote a paper which won the Research Paper Competition award at the 1994 ALISE meeting in Los Angeles. Its methods, concerns, and treatment are very similar in a number of respects to those reported in this and the following chapter, and it also incorporates Durrance's holistic, evaluative litmus test for determining transaction's effectiveness, i.e., a willingness to return to the same librarian with another, similar request.

Durrance, Dewdney, and Ross, like a host of earlier investigators, are concerned explicitly with the reference transaction, but, unlike the approach used here, do *not* deal with the readers' advisory transaction.

Please note that it is our assumption that the reference and the readers' advisory transactions are *not* the same phenomenon, even if, in some instances, they appear to be quite similar. Whether "reference transactions" are all only one kind of phenomenon or whether "readers' advisory" transactions are all examples of only one kind of phememon is not ruled on at this time. But it is assumed that reference transactions and readers' advisory transactions are different from each other.

A "readers' advisory transaction" is defined here as an exchange of information between two people with the purpose of one person's suggesting text for the other's later reading interest to one of them (although the advisor may also find new reading suggestions as a byproduct of the exchange). The text suggested in the transaction is expected to meet a recreational, emotional, psychological, or educational need. Unlike a reference transaction, the successful conclusion of a readers' advisory transaction is not the provision of a fact or missing data, nor does it attempt to fill a known gap in an otherwise complete informational or knowledge framework. The success of a readers' advisory transaction is reflected in a reader discovering a book (or cassette or software) which is enjoyable, entertaining, stimulating, mind-stretching, and eye-opening; it is in the realm of the subjective. On the other hand, the success of a reference transaction is reflected in the provision of a correct answer to an question or the filling of a gap in knowledge; it is in the realm of the objective.

An example may be helpful at this point. A friend, knowing of my disappointment that I had few opportunities to play Scrabble™, a game I like very much, suggested Scrabble™ software, which I have since added to my home computer. It has been a much-appreciated suggestion since I had not known that the game could be played in the absence of human players. It was a "readers'" advisory transaction. After my friend told me that it was available, I did not know how to procure it. The subsequent help I received in procuring the software was a reference phenomenon since I knew that it existed and was filling the gap in my knowledge of how to acquire a copy.

An attempt is made here to frame the research in such a way that it will provide baseline data establishing without regard to: (1) whether the individual receiving readers' advice is a child, young adult, or adult; (2) whether the advice given relates to individualized learning goals, expansion, and enrichment, or to assist readers in locating materials for pleasure; and (3) whether the material suggested is reading material, audio recording, video cassette, or software, etc.

Graduate students in my course, The Public Library, at North Carolina Central University visited various public libraries and subsequently filled out copies of a questionnaire on which the findings and tentative conclusions reported here are based. Much of what follows is excerpts or slightly edited versions of their narratives. Without their work, this research could not have taken place. It is assumed that their reports constitute a reasonably accurate reflection of what occurred. Their level of formal education and the investment in quality library service are presumably higher, on average, than in the American library clientele in the aggregate, but the technique used none-the-less permits the exploration to take place. The reported transactions occurred in county, independent municipal, and multicounty (regional system) public library settings. With one or two exceptions, all took place in North Carolina and all occurred between 1992 and 1994.

The focus of the questionnaire is what transpires when a client visits a library with the intention of finding a book like one he or she enjoyed earlier. The sample involved forty-three students; eleven students made two visits, making a total of fifty-four transactions reported. The sample is small and the visits were in a relatively small geographic area, especially if one is thinking in terms of practice in the United States. The work is exploratory and ground-breaking; not definitive. It is qualitative, not quantitative. I am looking for clues about the nature of the transaction and the nature of success and failure in Readers' Advisory Work. We hope that our explorations will stimulate others to follow up on our tentative conclusions and to explore new, related avenues and issues.

Phase I—*To Kill A Mockingbird*

The first phase took place in October 1992 and involved twelve graduate students who had all recently read—or reread—*To Kill a Mockingbird* by Harper Lee. The reasons for choosing this book were:

1. Lee wrote no other book and so the device of identifying other books by the same author was a strategy denied to the advisor.
2. This novel is a standard and hugely popular; it seemed realistic to assume that it would be widely known by public library staff members even if they had not actually read it themselves.
3. The book had been made into a very popular film, which further increased the likelihood that the title would not draw a blank when the student asked about it.

4. The book was not only a best seller when it first came out; it has subsequently been assigned widely for young adults in English classes.
5. The book's critical acclaim is perhaps best evidenced by the fact that it received a Pulitzer Prize for fiction.

Students each chose a different site to visit. Before asking for guidance, they were to ascertain whether they were speaking with a librarian. They were to use these words. "I would like to speak with a librarian, please. I want some help in choosing a book." At this point the attempt was made to explore readers' advisory transactions performed only by staff who have earned an M.L.S. This attempt was proven to be both intrusive and artificial, and was dropped from all later explorations. It is artificial because, as you will see, staff without the M.L.S. degree frequently deal with these questions even if the client specifically requests the help of a librarian. Furthermore, the "bottom line," from the point of view of library users, is what actually transpires in the library, not what might if all readers' advisory work were done by librarians.

The student questioners were asked to phrase their question in these words: "I enjoyed *To Kill a Mockingbird* and would like something else like it. Can you help me?" The literature discusses what should happen at this stage. For example, Mary Kay Chelton states,

As in the reference interview, you need to probe with open-ended questions to find out what the reader liked about a particular book or what other titles he or she has enjoyed recently. Restating the answers the reader that he or she has been heard: [for instance] "You enjoy Kay Scarpetta herself as much as the mysteries she solved."[4]

Baker suggests that although the readers' advisory interview is much like the reference interview, it may be "somewhat more complicated."[1]

But what happened to our questioners? In each case, they attempted to record the first response to the initial request in the original wording. Much was learned by including the step of asking to speak to a librarian. The individual who would like to speak to a librarian often approaches a circulation desk and speaks to a staff member who is not a librarian.

In other settings in which the public seeks expertise, patrons can identify professionals able to deal with their specialized needs. It is easy to distinguish the pharmacist from the assistants and the sales clerks in a drugstore; the dentist from the assistants in a dental office; the lawyer from the paralegals in the law office; and the doctors, nurses, and other specialists from each other and from the secretaries in a hospital. This was not the case in the public libraries visited by the students. It leads to an off-putting confusion on the part of the would-be advisees that is an unneccessary drain on perceived library effectiveness. Durrance, Dewdney, and Ross also write about this complication experienced by their students. Failure to identify staff qualified by virtue of education is a disservice to the people paying for qualifications.

The request to speak to a librarian brought a variety of inappropriate reactions on the part of *some* library assistants and *some* librarians, although this phenomenon was not prevalent. One student said that she "received a strange grin" from a woman who then glanced around the room. Then the woman said, "Well, okay, what is it you need?" Whether this woman was a librarian or not, the ambiguous response was perceived as inappropriate.

Another complication occurs from staff distraction, whether because they receive more requests than can be handled adequately by available staff members or because staff is expected to try to perform so many tasks that they cannot do all of them well. An example of this phenomenon occurred because, by law, public libraries in North Carolina are voter registration sites and this phase of the research took place in October, a time of widespread voter registration activity. Therefore, it is not surprising that two of the twelve investigators found that the staff was working with voter registration. In one of these two cases, the individual asked the student for the author's name and then replied "You can probably find his other books in the fiction section right over there." (The fact that Harper Lee's name is not gender specific had not occurred to the investigator until learning of this response.)

At the second site where voter registration undermined the effectiveness of library service offered, the questioner was sent from the circulation area to a reference desk. After a wait, a librarian, perhaps trying to handle too many requests at once, heard the question, turned away from the advisee to a computer, and said aloud "1959." She started a search. After a few minutes, she turned back to the student (or "advisee") and asked if she would like to read more on civil rights. That gave the student an opportunity to correct the misapprehension of the advisor, saying that it was the Southern atmosphere that she had liked about the book. (Note that although the librarian did not explicitly probe, the advisee felt that the possibility of politely interjecting helpful information was at long last appropriate.) At this point, the librarian jumped up and went to the stacks, indicating that she should be followed. She pulled off *Raney* as the first of several books, talking while walking. The student ended up with titles by Ann Siddons, Josephine Humphrey, and Lee Smith, in additon to Clyde Edgerton's *Raney*.

But in this case, the advisee was dissatisfied with the service performed, gave the transaction low grades, and would not choose to return even though at some level the service seemed satisfactory in that it provided her with several possibly appropriate books to read. The problem occurred in the execution of the transaction: unexplained turning away from the advisee to a computer; rapid, unexplained movement into stacks; and total absence of any "stackside manner." This provides evidence that the way a library staff member interacts with users is important, perhaps more important than the job actually done in any particular transaction—a point stressed by Durrance, Dewdney, and Ross in connection with reference service.

The conclusion that courteous attention was possibly even more important than results kept coming up in the discussions students had about their interviews when we discussed their findings during class sessions. If the advisee gets appropriate books to read but never wants to repeat the experience, the transaction is a serious loss from the point of view of sound library service and good client relations.

It was not only voter registration that got in the way of paying attention to a readers' advisory question. In another case, the library assistant asked the student who wrote the book, looked up the name in the catalog and said that "he" had not written other books. This assistant said that a second employee could help but that she was busy with a group of school children. After waiting 20 minutes with no further communication, the student left.

We can conclude from these cases that would-be advisees cannot determine necessarily:

- where in a public library reading advice should be sought;
- whether they are speaking to a librarian or not; and,
- in some instances, whether the staff is available for providing such advice within a reasonable time period.

But even if the librarian is located and makes appropriate recommendations, the advisee may still be completely dissatisfied by the abrupt, abstract, and mechanical manner of the readers' advisor. Such deficiencies need to be addressed by library management in order for readers' advisory service to take place effectively.

Let us turn now to the narrative account of the highest-ranked transaction in this group. In this case, the advisee (Caucasian) approached a circulation desk and asked to speak to a librarian. The staff member (Arican American), not a librarian herself, reached for the phone, presumably to summon a librarian. When the advisee added that she wanted help in choosing a book, the staff member hung up the phone and asked what kind of help was needed. To the standard question about wanting something like *To Kill a Mockingbird*, the assistant responded, "Then you will want to read *A Time to Kill* by Grisham, John Grisham; it's the closest thing to *To Kill a Mockingbird.*" (If you've read both novels, I think you will agree that there are a good number of similarities—as there are in some other senses—in another Grisham book, *The Client.*)

But, good guess or not, the advisor did not attempt to find out what the advisee liked about the book at this stage. If, for example, the advisee enjoyed the sensitive treatment of a girl's growing intellectual and emotional maturity as shown in her relationship with her father, brother, and friends, the recommendation would have been a distinctly "false hit." If what the advisee liked about *Mockingbird* is the theme of the high cost of purchasing one's own integrity and its effect on one's family, the fit is not good either.

The assistant then determined that *A Time to Kill* was on reserve and so was not available anyway. Interrupted by another user, she in-

> **Figure 1.   Authors mentioned in responses to a request for something "like" Harper Lee's *To Kill a Mockingbird*.**
>
> 1. Grisham, John (2 mentions)
> 2. McCullers, Carson (2 mentions)
> 3. Smith, Lee (2 mentions)
> 4. Baldwin, James
> 5. Bridges, Sue Ellen
> 6. Caudle, Neil
> 7. Clark, Mary Higgins
> 8. du Maurier, Daphne
> 9. Edgerton, Clyde
> 10. Francis, Dick
> 11. Himes, Chester
> 12. Humphrey, Josephine
> 13. Hurston, Zora Neale
> 14. King, Stephen
> 15. Lauber, Lynn
> 16. Leedom-Ackerman, Joanne
> 17. Lord, Bette Bao
> 18. McCollough, Colleen
> 19. McCorkle, Jill
> 20. Minet, Susan
> 21. Naylor, Gloria
> 22. Oke, Janette
> 23. Siddons, Anne
> 24. Walker, Alice

dicated—in a nice example of good client relations—that while she helped someone else, the advisee should look at books with an identifying label on their spines (she later explained that this symbol designated that the book was either written by a African-American author or was about African-Americans' experience.) She soon reappeared at the advisee's side and recommended other authors and titles on the basis of obviously extensive personal knowledge. This kind of knowledge is very widely mentioned in the literature as an invaluable tool of the trade of readers' advisors.

At this point, the advisee began to think that the advisor was "recommending any titles that dealt with the 1920s or 1930s [and] that dealt with black experience, such as Chester Himes' *Cotton Comes to*

Figure 2. Titles mentioned in response to a request for something "like" *To Kill a Mockingbird*.

---

 1. *Member of the Wedding* (Mentioned twice)
 2. *A Time to Kill* (Mentioned twice)
 3. *Cotton Comes to Harlem*
 4. *Ferris Beach*
 5. *The Grass Crown*
 6. *The Heart is a Lonely Hunter*
 7. *The Ladies of Misa Lorch*
 8. *The Lake Town Rebellion*
 9. *Monkeys*
10. *No Marble Angels*
11. *Quincunx*
12. *Rebecca*
13. *Roses for Momma*
14. *A Separate Peace*
15. *Spring Moon*
16. *Their Eyes Were Watching God*
17. *Three Complete Novels and Five Short Stories* [Daphne du Maurier]
18. *Voices from Home*
19. *White Girls*

Harlem." It was at this point that the advisor, presumably sensitive to the body language of the advisee, asked what the advisee liked about *Mockingbird*. Finally, the advisee was prompted to state that she "liked the setting—in the South—and that it showed the awakening in the awareness of whites that blacks were being treated unfairly." The advisor then moved to the shelves and, on the basis of knowledge of the library's fiction collection, suggested Zora Neale Hurston's *Their Eyes Were Watching God* and *The Laketown Rebellion*, Lynn Lauber's *White Girls*, and Joanne Leedom-Ackerman's *No Marble Angles*.

This was the only case in this phase of research in which a student awarded the highest rating possible to the advisor in all three characteristics rated on the questionnaire: A) knowledge, B) professionalism, and C) attention to the request. The student also indicated that she would, if convenient, return for further advice from this advisor.

This article has described the best and worst of these twelve cases. Viewing these transactions as responses to a single stimulus, it is interesting to note the range of titles and authors readers were advised to read. The twelve visits led to the suggestion that twenty-five unique authors are like Harper Lee, plus eight more on a supplemental list provided to one advisee. Furthermore, twenty unique titles were suggested, not counting the eight on the list provided. Figures 1 and 2 show the responses to the single readers' advisory question asked by these twelve individuals in different public libraries.

Phase II—*The Color Purple*

In part because the graduate students conducting these interviews were both African American and white, I thought that we—the students and I—might discover something of value about the dynamics of readers' advisory by including a work by an African-American author similar in stature to Harper Lee's *Mockingbird*. Alice Walker's *The Color Purple* was our choice; it also reflected personal taste since I very much enjoyed both of these novels.

Like *Mockingbird*, *The Color Purple* is a standard and hugely popular work that was also made into a popular film. It was a best seller and is found on many recommended reading lists. Furthermore, it won a Pulitzer Prize for fiction. The only major difference from the point of view of readers' advisory is that Walker has written many other books. That fact allowed an advisor the opportunity to suggest that the advisee could read other works by this author, which is a relatively easy way to handle, or at least to begin to handle, a readers' advisory transaction.

Depending on the different students' reading histories, the route the transaction would take from this starting point would diverge: If the advisee had already read the other titles by Alice Walker available in the library at that time, the path would turn to other authors and resemble the situation in the *Mockingbird* phases of the research; if the advisee was open to further Walker books, the transaction might then come to a satisfactory close.

Let's start with most successful transaction among the eleven in this phase. In this case, top grades were given for knowledge, professionalism, and attention to the advisee's request. Although the advisee hesitated because she likes to browse and felt "rushed by the staff," she decided that she would return for advice on further reading after her experience. This case illustrates dynamics that can occur in the fairly common team approach to a readers' advisory question in a public library—an approach that several narratives indicate seem to help get the creative juices flowing, or, as one student wrote, to "jump start" a staff member's suggestions. Since the reading interests and memories of each employee differ, it seems to be an appropriate, if often impossible or excessively lavish, strategy to utilize.

When the advisee asked to speak with a librarian, the woman behind the desk hesitated. When the advisee indicated that she wanted help choosing a book, the advisor (we'll call her Ann) said, "I can try to help you; what do you need?"

"I liked *The Color Purple*," said the advisee.

"Ahh," was the reply.

Ann seemed at a loss for words and began moving toward the fiction section: all readers' advisors know that sinking feeling. She turned to two other staff members who were not engaged in helping anyone else and said, "She wants something like *The Color Purple*."

The second staff member (we'll call her Ruth) asked the advisee, "Have you read her new book?"

Ann broke in with, "Alice Walker is the author of *The Color Purple*."

Ruth picked up Walker's new book, *Possessing the Secret of Joy*, to show it to the advisee. A third woman (let's call her Doris) came up and said, "But that's not really like *The Color Purple*; it's strange." Doris made further comments about characters—comments that the advisee could not recall when she recorded the transaction.

At this point, Ruth asked, "What did you like about *The Color Purple*?" This was an all-too-rare instance of probing about the emotional and psychological space occupied by the advisee. The advisee replied, "I liked the strength of the female characters and how they worked together to overcome adversity." Doris pulled Fannie Flagg's *Fried Green Tomatoes at the Whistle-Stop Cafe* and said that she was sure the advisee would like it.

Doris and Ann began talking between themselves: "That was a good choice!" "She should like that book." "Yes, give her that one." (The pep talk should have been withheld while the advisee was present, because it tended both to create premature closure and also to exclude the advisee.)

From this point on, the details of new book loan periods, getting a library card, and library hours were quickly dealt with. The entire transaction took about five minutes. As indicated above, the advisee felt rushed by the "overefficient manner" of the three advisors and would have wanted to be free to browse and not feel that the job was done and that she was now expected to exit with the recommended title. Nonetheless, this case was rated the best of the lot.

At this point, let's look at another aspect of the transactions—an aspect which raises very different issues around the provision of good readers' advisory service: The unintended, probably well-meaning racial stereotyping that went on in some instances. With both *To Kill a Mockingbird* and *The Color Purple*, there was a potential for the subject matter of the novels, the race, and the gender of both the advisee and the advisor to come into play in ways that reflect stereotyping rather than what is actually said.

In the following case, there is something that seems curious, even though the African-American female advisee succeeded in getting suggestions for further reading that she might enjoy and concluded that she would come back for more advice. The white library assistant, explaining that the librarian was not in, offered to help. On hearing the request, she replied, "I am sorry, but I have never read *The Color Purple*. And I'm not familiar with black authors. But if you could give me a few minutes I will try to find you some authors."

The assistant was courteous, honest, and made an effort to provide assistance, but if the advisee had been white or Hispanic, would the remark about familiarity with African-American authors have been made? No white or African-American students asking for *To Kill a Mockingbird* were told the advisor did not read white authors or were given lists of white authors as a response. Note that it is an assumption that the advisee wants authors to be African-American and that fact alone will suffice. Nothing was said about what the advisee liked about the book, so the assumption seems totally unwarranted. Depending on what the student liked about *The Color Purple*, Amy Tan's *The Joy Luck Club* or Lee Smith's *Fair and Tender Ladies* might have been good suggestions and, most probably, far better than what, as we are about to see, was offered to her.

Figure 3. Authors mentioned in response to a request for something "like" Alice Walker's *The Color Purple*.

1. McMillan, Terri (Mentioned six times)
2. Morrison, Toni (Mentioned five times)
3. Naylor, Gloria (Mentioned twice)
4. Angelou, Maya
5. Baldwin, James
6. Cooper, J. California
7. Edgerton, Clyde
8. Flagg, Fannie
9. Gibbons, Kaye
10. Kinsolver, B.
11. Maron, Margaret
12. McCorkle, Jill
13. Parks [no first name given]
14. Sanders, Diane
15. Siddons, Anne

The assistant told the advisee where the novels were located and asked her to browse. According to the student, it was approximately fifteen minutes later that the assistant returned and said that some good African-American authors were Terry McMillan and Alice Walker and provided titles in each case. She mentioned that J. California Cooper was an African-American author and, if the advisee was interested in African-American male authors, James Baldwin could be tried.

The advisee, curious about the source of these suggestions, asked the assistant where she had gotten them. The assistant replied that a staff member reads a lot of African-American authors and told her that a reader might enjoy them.

The following case is included not because it is typical and certainly not because it is in any respect good practice. It may not even offer insights to improve service. But it does have this virtue: I'll bet you're doing better than this at your shop!

Incidently, the advisee was white and female and the staff members who dealt with this transaction were both females—one white and one African American. The first woman asked if she could help the advisee. The advisee indicated she would like to speak to a librar-

---

Figure 4. Titles mentioned in response to something "like" Alice Walker's *The Color Purple*.

1. *Women of Brewster Place* (3 mentions)
2. *Bailey's Cafe* (2 mentions)
3. *Mame* (2 mentions)
4. *Possessing the Secret of Joy* (2 mentions)
5. *Beloved*
6. *Clover*
7. *Cold Sassy Tree*
8. *Color Struck*
9. *A Cure for Dreams*
10. *Disappearing Act*
11. *Fried Green Tomatoes at the Whistle-Stop Cafe*
12. *Homemade Love*
13. *Jazz*
14. *Learning Tree*
15. *Linden Hills*
16. *Love Story Black*
17. *Maura Day*
18. *Outer Banks*
19. *Sophia's Choice*
20. *Tar Baby*
21. *Temple of My Familiar*
22. *Waiting to Exhale*
23. *The Wall of the Plague*
24. *You Can't Keep a Good Woman Down*

---

ian. The woman hesitated, looked puzzled, and said to the other assistant, "She would like to talk to the librarian."

The second woman looked worried and said, "That's not me."

The first replied "You're next highest-ranking person here." (Try to imagine a parallel situation occuring when you ask for a pharmacist at a drugstore or anywhere else that you specifically ask for the services of a trained professional.)

The second woman came over and asked what was wanted and was told the advisee wanted help in finding a book. The advisee wrote that at this point, "She looked at me as if I was from outer space." The advisee continued by saying she wanted something like *The Color Purple*. In the meantime, the assistant had turned her back to the advisee to write something for another client. She whipped her head around and said very suspiciously, "You want a black book?"

The student, apparently feeling the need to explain herself, said that she liked the way the women bonded in the book. The assistant pointed toward the OPAC and said, "Go over there and type in 'Women Bonding and Women Bondage.'"

The student did so. The assistant hollered over to look for "Rooster something"—the advisee didn't hear the words clearly.

The second assistant, apparently feeling badly about the way things were going, came over to the catalog and attempted to help. The first assistant hollered to look in the "subject book," by which she meant *Subject Guide to Books in Print*. It, of course, was of no help in this case. The student noted in her account, but did not remark to the assistant, that *Fiction Catalog*, a source that might have helped, was beneath it in same range of books. The second assistant then mentioned some books she had read about "sturdy women" and suggested that the advisee return when the reference librarian was in. I like to believe, borrowing and twisting some words from a well-known advertisement, that it doesn't get any worse than this.

As to the responses to the single stimulus of *The Color Purple*, the eleven visits called to mind fifteen authors and twenty-four titles, not including a "Southern Accents" list of fifty-three authors and 107 titles handed to one advisee. The "Southern Accents" list is a response that might be welcome, as it was in this case, or constitute an information overload.

Phase III—Personal Favorites

During the early stages of this exploratory research into the reference transaction, our approach was to have all the students ask about the same titles, which were chosen by me. The advantage was that we could compare various responses to a single book, thus establishing that readers' advisors suggest a multitude of titles and authors all allegedly "like" the one mentioned by the patron. We also learned that an extraordinary range of behaviors and approaches occur in public libraries as staff members attempt to deal with the complex and difficult challenge presented when asked to provide a book like one read and enjoyed earlier.

In the following cases, students selected books that *they* especially enjoyed during the past few years. They were also asked to reflect on why they enjoyed the books and to write an account of their reflections. Isn't the motive for readers' advisory transactions the fond memory of reading a book and the attempt to replicate that experience? This seems a reasonable working hypothesis to this investigator.

In this phase, thirty-one students visited North Carolina public libraries asking Readers' Advisory questions during 1993 and 1994. The issues raised during class discussions following their visits under these revised conditions were largely the same as those in Phase I. In fact, these issues were similar to those metioned by Dewdney and Ross, who write about students who took *reference questions* of genuine interest to them and reported in narratives what occurred:

> . . . Four themes occurred in these narratives: The lack of identifying cues by which professional librarians could be identified; the choice by 55 percent of staff members to accept the user's initial question at face value and not to conduct a reference interview; search failure following unmonitored referrals; and the omission of follow-up questions in two thirds of the transactions.[5]

We saw in Phase I how difficult it was for most of the advisees to determine whether professional librarians were dealing with their transactions. A readers' advisory transaction that included asking what the advisee liked about the book occurred less than 25 percent of the time in this research; indeed, in several of the narratives we learn that information about why they liked a book was initiated by advisees, not advisors, even though they indicated that the advisor asked them what they liked about the book. Failure to monitor advisees' success was common as was the omission of follow-up questions.

What was learned from these self-generated readers' advisory questions? Again let us look for insights by selectively examining the advisees' records of their experiences.

The following account is a nearly perfect textbook example of a transaction that began with the request for a book like John Grisham's *The Firm*. In this case, the staff member responded, "Yes, I think I know several that would be that same type—have you ever read anything by Scott Turow?" After consulting the OPAC to see whether a specific title was in that day, the staff member led the advisee to the fiction collection and began to inquire as to why she had liked *The Firm*. Specific questions the librarian asked her were: (1) "Which Grisham novel did you read?"; (2) "What did you like about it?"; (3) "Have you ever used this library before?"; (4) "Have you ever read anything by . . . ?"; (5) "Have you read any of Grisham's other novels?"; and (6) "Do you think you will be able to find these books [the ones she recommended] in the stacks?"

The student awarded the adviser top grades on a seven-point scale for: (a) knowledgeability, (b) professionalism, and (c) attention to the request. She also indicated she would return to this librarian for advice on further reading.

An inquiry by the staff advisers into why the advisee liked the book occurred in this case but, as we noted above, occurred in less than one quarter of the total cases. Chelton explicitly recommends finding out what advisees liked about the book in her advice on the way to conduct a readers' advisory interview.

Tentatively, it appears that, along with an open, attentive manner, all readers' advisory service should include a question about *why* the user liked the book. First, it clarifies what other books and authors will appeal to the reader's emotional, psychological, or learning needs and second, it seems to be uniformly well received. Readers appear to like to talk about the enjoyment they received from a well-liked book. It seems to be one of the values of readers' advisory service in and of itself without regard to whether any useful recommendations occur during the transaction. Reading is such a solitary activity that readers have few opportunities to express why they like what they like; the expression of recollected reading pleasure and the sharing of that pleasure with the staff appears to enhance user satisfaction—satisfaction with both the staff member who asks the question and listens attentively to the answer and also with the library.

Indeed, the student narratives and class discussions make it seem likely that the readers' advisory transaction is *not* about how similar the text of Book A is to the text of Book B, although the literature about it and those conducting such transactions act as though that is the case.

Successful readers' advisory transactions are about relating Reader A's experience with Book A to the likelihood that Reader A would value the experience of reading Book B. While the point may at first be a subtle distinction of small value, it may lie at the crux of the phenomenon. In a few narratives, the readers' advisors seem to show an implicit awareness of this distinction: Some said that although a recommended book was different from the one an advisee asked about, they were nonetheless sure the advisee would like it. However, in only some of the cases was their assuredness based on an exchange about the advisee's preferences and other clues. In other cases it seems based on the advisor's projection of personal likes and dislikes, which is of doubtful value. An egregious example of the later case came with the recommendation, in the absence of probing that an individual who liked *To Kill a Mockingbird* would certainly like *A Separate Peace*. The latter is a somber tale about young men in a New England private school; while both books are sensitive, coming-of-age stories in America—and I certainly liked both of them—the suggestion did seem to come "out of the thin blue air."

The observation that advisors ought to concern themselves with probes about why the advisee likes a book raises the question of whether there seems to be a positive relationship between such an inquiry and whether an advisee would wish to return for further advice. The tentative answer is a resounding "Yes." Only thirteen of the fifty-three reports included an inquiry about why they liked a book. Of these cases, eleven also had usable answers concerning whether the advisee would like to return for further advice from this staff member. Of these eleven, nine (82 percent) said they would return. (This compares with only 62 percent who would return to reader's advisors in the group as a whole.) Efforts should be made to replicate elsewhere and for much larger samples this aspect of the research.

In the next chapter, this line of research is continued in an effort to explore how children's readers' advisory is handled in public libraries.

Notes

1. Baker, Sharon. "Readers' Advisory Services: A Call for More Research." *RQ* 32 (Winter 1992): 167.

2. Shearer, Kenneth, and Pauletta Bracy. "Readers' Advisory Services: A Response to the the Call for More Research." *RQ* 33 (Summer 1994): 456-459.

3. Durrance, Joan. "Reference Service: Does the 55 Percent Rule Tell the Whole Story?" *Library Journal* (April 15, 1989): 31-36.

4. Chelton, Mary K. "Read Any Good Books Lately? Helping Patrons Find What They Want." *Lj* (May 1, 1993): 34.

5. Dewdney, Patricia, and Catherine Sheldrick Ross. "Flying a Light Aircraft: Reference Service Evaluation from a User's Viewpoint." *RQ* (Winter, 1994): 217-230.

Chapter Two:
The Nature of the Readers' Advisory Transaction in Children's and Young Adult Reading

by Pauletta Brown Bracy

$\mathcal{M}$ost often when one considers readers' advisory work in children's and young adult library services, the focus is on connecting the reader to the literature in meaningful ways that foster cognitive as well as psychological and social development. This definition of purpose thus embraces two perspectives in examining the connection. In the first instance, those in the field of reading concern themselves with what has been traditionally termed "Reader Response." Analyzing the reading process, reading scholar L. M. Rosenblatt has attempted to describe the literary transaction by defining and delineating efferent reading and aesthetic reading. In the former, the child reader must learn to focus on extracting the public meaning of the text; in aesthetic reading, the child reader must learn to draw on more of the experiential matrix—including the personal, the qualitative, kinesthetic, sensuous inner resonances of the words.[1]

A. N. Applebee designed a systematic, integrated model that illustrates major developmental stages in the formulation of response among children and adolescents through adulthood.[2] The range begins with the propensity of young respondents to retell a story in whole or in part. This stage is followed by an ability to summarize. Then, during early through middle adolescence, analysis of the structure of the work can occur. Finally, the mode of thinking shifts to generalization, the most mature mode of response. Individuals at this stage are able to articulate abstract statements about theme and meaning of a particular work.[3]

Many have attempted to scrutinize the variables accounting for developmental differences. As an example, Beach and Wendler considered developmental differences in readers' responses in a study that compared inferences about characters in a literary work among eighth graders, college freshmen, and seniors. These inferences were rated according to social and psychological meanings. The researchers confirmed the existence of differences among the groups in cognitive development, social cognition, and self-concepts in their examination of the influences of beliefs, perceptions, and long-range goals.[4]

The second perspective involves librarianship. Librarians investigated reading among patrons as early as the first quarter of the twentieth century with the most common approach on discussion around books rather than people.[5] For children's reading, emphasis was placed on reading interests and habits.[6]

Chelton has documented early young adult services as a specialty concept in the public library that emerged as a way to bridge the gap for early adolescents between the smaller, more personalized, and protected children's rooms and the open ranges of the adult department. In the public libraries of Cleveland and New York, separate rooms were designated and, more specifically, Enoch Pratt Free Library of Baltimore employed a trained readers' advisor for young adults.[7] Chelton also recognized the strong roots of young adult services in the traditional readers' advisory function of public libraries.

Another individual who has considered readers' advisory services for young adults is Patrick Jones, who offered the five following goals of readers' advisory services:

1. Match YA reading interests with the library collection.
2. Provide access to the library collection.
3. Learn the likes/dislikes of the YA readers.
4. Promote reading through the use of documents.
5. Find the right book for the right YA at the right time for the right reason.[8]

These five principles, which reiterate the purpose of matching the reader and the literature, can also be applied to readers' advisory services for children.

In a discussion of readers' advisory for young adults, Lundin suggested that services for youth can best be understood in terms of four questions: (a) What happens in the literary experience?; (b) What is young adult literature?; (c) Who are the young adults?; and (d) How can we as librarians best serve this important constituency?[9] Again, this set of guidelines can be applied to work with children. However, one significant distinction does exist. In cases of readers' advisory services involving children, adult caregivers often enter transactions on behalf of children. In contrast, young adults usually act on their own behalf and present their requests themselves.

The 1990 national survey of children's services and resources in public libraries, based on data collected 1988–1989 confirmed the widespread practice of readers' advisory in children's library services. Ninety-three percent of the libraries in the survey reported that the services were offered, ranked closely behind summer reading programs and study space.[10]

The 1988 companion study, which dealt with young adult services, ranked readers' advisory services third at 88 percent behind first ranked study space (94 percent) and ranked college and career information second (92 percent).[11]

For the most part, librarianship has not scrutinized the readers' advisory transaction involving children's and young adult literature. The research foci to date have been on developmental responses in reading from the investigators in the field of reading, and on reading interests among patrons from the researchers in librarianship. The following report of qualitative research presents case study analyses of transactions between adult patrons who sought advice in children's and young adult literature and the library staff members who attempted to respond to their needs.

The Design

During the academic semesters of 1992–1994 a total of twenty-seven graduate students enrolled in the North Carolina Central University School of Library and Information Sciences participated in a study designed to examine the nature of the readers' advisory transaction involving children's and young adult literature. In two phases of the study, students were directed to visit a public library of choice and initiate the readers' advisory transaction by requesting assistance in identifying a book or books to read similar to a title previously read. With one exception, all libraries visited by the students were located in North Carolina.

In Phase I, all students were told to identify the book of reference as *Roll of Thunder, Hear My Cry* by Mildred Taylor. This book was selected because of its Newbery Medal status and also because it is the second title in the historical fiction trilogy about the southern African American Logan family during the post-Depression era. Another consideration was to name a book which reflected an ethnic perspective to also determine the impact of this variable in an otherwise typical transaction. Taylor's book also continues to enjoy profitable sales and is destined to become a classic in children's literature. In addition, it is cited in numerous bibliographic sources as an outstanding work with appeal for both children and young adults. It also appears quite frequently on lists as required reading in language arts curricula. Hence, the expectation was that this book and its ethnic context would be well known in library circles.

Phase II was guided by the same procedure but differed in that students could select any children's or young adult literature of interest. It is not unusual for those reading young adult fiction to also seek titles of adult fiction with young adult appeal. The American Library Association's annual list of "Best Books for Young Adults" does identify adult fiction and nonfiction that has a potential young adult audience. In this phase, some titles known as adult fiction were selected by the students.

The discussion that follows is organized according to these two phases.

Phase I: Roll of Thunder, Hear My Cry

In the first phase, eight student patrons (hereafter referred to as patrons) who presented the titles to public library staff members—both librarians and other personnel (hereafter referred to as librarians)—

and the patrons' experiences are described. Examination of each particular case revealed patterns of conduct in the transactions worthy of consideration. Responses to the question, "I enjoyed *Roll of Thunder, Hear My Cry* and would like to read something else like it. Can you help me?" were varied although levels of satisfaction were rather consistent. Patrons were asked to rate the overall experience on a scale of one to seven, ranging from "very satisfied" to "not at all satisfied" in areas of librarian's knowledgeability, professionalism, and attention to the request. Those responses that fell in the middle range were considered to reflect moderate satisfaction.

Most were favorably impressed with the attention to their requests, and all patrons found satisfaction with the librarian's knowledge and professionalism. One patron was quite disappointed in knowledgeability, but was moderately satisfied in the other two areas.

All were asked if they would return to this librarian for advice on further reading. Six indicated that they would do so.

To further explore the nature of the transaction, an examination of the initial response to the patron inquiry is important as an early indicator of the patron's satisfaction with the transaction. Typically, as suggested earlier, parents and/or caregivers may act on behalf of children in the readers' advisory transaction. In one case, the initial inquiry was modified to: "My daughter enjoyed *Roll of Thunder, Hear My Cry*. I'd like to find another book like it to buy as a Christmas gift." The librarian's response was, "How old is your daughter?" Another patron spoke on behalf of her son and explained that he enjoyed the book and that she wanted a similar title as a recommendation. That librarian responded in a similar manner with, "What age is your son?" These two reactions to the request reflected the librarians' knowledge and concern for readability as one guideline in meeting the needs of the reader.

The librarians both followed through with consideration of reading level, respectively asking if the female child was reading at or above her reading level and suggesting that the male child could read on a higher level. Another similarity was apparent. Both librarians began to explore genre preferences—contemporary or historical fiction—and reading interests as inherent in the question, "Does he have any particular interests like baseball or soccer?"

Familiarity with the literature was reflected in the librarian's response ("That was a Newbery winner") in another case. This librarian followed with an introduction to the library's holdings of Newbery titles, pointing to books on the shelves. Eventually, she moved on to the author, Taylor, assuming that the patron wanted to read other works by the author. Lastly, the patron was instructed on how to scan the juvenile section searching for "TAY" on the spines of the shelved books.

In one other case, the initial reaction ("By her?") also assumed the patron's preference of authorship although it was the beginning probe question that allowed the patron an opportunity to focus the transaction and guide the librarian. The patron's affirmative response led the librarian to recommend other titles by Taylor and, ultimately, other African American authors.

Speaking of authorship, one patron was asked to confirm the authorship and setting in the initial response: "Who is the author of that? Was it set in the 1800s?" Again, some familiarity with the title is reflected in the second part of the response. Moving toward the card catalog, the librarian probed for the book's appeal and eventually confirmed that the theme was what the patron liked about the book. Evidently, the librarian was not very familiar with children's literature, as she sought assistance from a colleague who recommended one other children's author and two authors of adult literature—all African American. Setting was dropped once theme was determined to be the appeal, but that literary element was erroneously and unduly equated with ethnicity of authorship in the librarian's attempt to complete the transaction.

Two unfortunate initial responses were disturbing. The remark "I'm not sure I know what you are talking about" preceded a trip to the card catalog and a search for Taylor (following the patron's identification of the author for the librarian). The fruitless search (no holdings by Mildred Taylor were discovered in the collection) precipitated an apology and a report from the patron that the librarian made "no further move to help me." In the other case, the response was a question for the patron: "What have you done first, come to the desk?" Eventually, probing about the appeal occurred in the question of "Are you looking for a book with blacks in it?" A "Not necessarily, I just liked the book. . ." response by the patron yielded a referral to booklists of varied titles that middle school students read for an annual literary competition. The patron was directed to peruse the lists so that she "might find something similar" and to "give them back when you finish." The librarian left the patron with no further interaction.

Probing began immediately in only one case. The initial response to the inquiry focused on the likes and dislikes about the book and also queries about interest in the author. After checking the OPAC to discern availability of the author's works, the librarian also consulted reference sources and continued to probe likes and dislikes about the literary elements, including setting. Not surprisingly, the patron rated the overall experience at the greatest level of satisfaction, ranking it number one in all three areas—one of two patrons to do so.

This case is considered to be the optimum in how the transaction should be conducted by the librarian. Characteristically, the thorough probing was followed by a wide array of appropriate recommended titles and authors and consultation of bibliographic tools. The patron's report does not reflect readability, but the titles are comparable in reading level. Also significant is the patron's description of the librarian's attitude and body language: "She was very warm . . . body language was very positive and encouraging. . ."

Examining the ultimate desirable outcome of pertinent and useful identified titles, it is interesting to note those titles and authors recommended by the librarians. These are shown in Tables I and II. Special designations to highlight certain characteristics follow some titles. A few titles and authors were cited in more than one case; numbers indicate frequency of those recommendations.

In half of the cases, the third book of the Taylor trilogy, *Let the Circle Be Unbroken*, was recommended; the first, *Song of the Trees*, was never mentioned. Librarians pursued another of the author's works, *Road to Memphis*, or sought to maintain the readers' interest in the family saga by recommending the other two titles in the trilogy. And, as can be noted, a number of the titles represent children's literature portraying the African American experience. Overall, children's titles were mostly recommended, but some of the connections to *Roll of Thunder, Hear My Cry* leave much to speculation. *Temple of My Familiar* by Alice Walker, along with *Mules and Men* by Zora Neale Hurston, are clearly adult titles and were perhaps suggested by indi-

TABLE I: Recommended Titles for *Roll of Thunder, Hear My Cry**		
Recommended Titles	Frequency	Notes
Let the Circle Be Unbroken	4	T; AE
MC Higgins, The Great	2	AE
Teetoncey	2	
Anastasia (series)	1	
The Autobiography of Miss Jane Pittman	1	AAA
Bridge to Terabithia	1	
Computer Nut	1	
A Day No Pigs Would Die	1	
A Different Kind of Christmas	1	
The Education of Little Tree	1	
Great Eggspectations of Lila Fenwick	1	
Island of the Blue Dolphins	1	
Mules and Men	1	AAA
Mystery of Drear House	1	AE
Road to Memphis	1	TO; AE
Slave Dancer	1	AE
Sounder	1	AE
Sugar Blue	1	
Summer of My German Soldier	1	
Sweet Whispers, Brother Rush	1	AE
Temple of My Familiar	1	AAA
Thank You, Dr. Martin Luther King, Jr.	1	AE
Where the Red Fern Grows	1	
Zeely	1	AE

*NOTES: T (Taylor Title in the Trilogy)
TO (Taylor Title Other Than Trilogy)
AE (African American Experience for Children)
AAA (African American Experience for Adults)
Numbers following titles denote frequency.

viduals who knew of "black titles" and had no regard for the distinction between children's literature and literature for adults.

This phenomenon of "ethnic elicitation" (used by this researcher to describe recommendations based on ethnic experiences of the same ethnic group or authors of the same ethnic group) was more apparent in the wide array of recommended authors. Of the African American authors in Table II, only four are known for writing

TABLE II: Recommended Authors for Mildred Taylor's *Roll of Thunder, Hear My Cry**		
Recommended Authors	Frequency	Notes
Virginia Hamilton	2	AE
J. Byars	I	
Vera Cleaver	I	
Paula Fox	I	
Ernest Gaines	I	AAA
Bette Greene	I	
Alex Haley	I	AAA
Zora Neale Hurston	I	AAA
Lois Lowry	I	
Terry McMillan	I	AAA
J. McMullen	I	
Walter Dean Myers	I	AE
Scott O'Dell	I	
Wilson Rawls	I	
Ntozake Shange	I	AAA
Eleanora Tate	I	AE
Mildred Taylor	I	AE
Alice Walker	I	AAA

*NOTES: AE (African American Children's/Young Adult Author)
              AAA (African American Author of Adult Fiction)
              Numbers following authors denote frequency.

children's and/or young adult literature, including Taylor. One could argue that possibly the African American adult authors were recommended because children are encouraged to and do read beyond their levels and interests, but adult situations as presented in books by Ntozake Shange, Terry McMillan, and Ernest Gaines, for example, emphatically are not for children. Although it is conceded that Gaines and Walker may appear on senior high school English reading lists, they definitely are considered to be writers of adult fiction.

Virginia Hamilton, an established author who was recommended twice, is well known for writing about the African American experience for children and young adults. She and Mildred Taylor are the only two African American children's authors who have won the Newbery Medal for their works. African American writer Walter Dean

Myers, who was also recommended, has received the Margaret Edwards Award for distinction in young adult literature.

In terms of other practices, most often no consultation of published sources occurred. In the two cases in which other resources were involved, the bibliographic titles, *Our Family, Our Friends, Our World* (Bowker) and *Your Reading* (NCTE) were used, and they are appropriate tools in children's and young adult services. Also, a locally prepared list of children's books was consulted in another case. For the most part, librarians made no referrals to other staff members who may have been able to assist in meeting the patron needs.

In one case in which the librarian suggested titles on bases other than patron personal preferences; staff personal knowledge; and consultation of the collection, other staff, or published sources, the librarian suggested all the titles written by Mildred Taylor in the collection.

A general assessment of these few cases leads to the unsettling conclusion that in spite of the generally adequate levels of satisfaction with the assistance rendered in the transactions, the cases do not reveal consistently good service reflective of sound probing and reasonable consultation of pertinent sources. Instead, these cases are fraught with assumptions made by staff, which are exercises in speculation and which serve to undermine the primary goal of readers' advisory services. Readers' advisory services should focus on the patron's needs and not inadvertently impose an obtrusive bias of staff that may result in an unsuccessful transaction.

Phase II: Titles of Choice

Again, patrons were most often moderately satisfied with knowledgeability of the librarian, professionalism of the librarian, and attention paid to the request. The greatest frequency in the low/no satisfaction range occurred in the area of attention to request and was closely followed by the knowlegeability factor.

Table III contains a synopsis of each case, including titles presented to the librarians along with recommended titles and authors. In those instances in which no information is presented, patrons reported that no recommendations were made.

In these cases, which involved mostly young adult fiction, the patrons' initial and final contacts were most often with reference librar-

TABLE III: Recommended Titles and Authors
             Patron Titles of Choice of Children's and Young Adult
             Titles

Patron Title	Suggested Titles	Suggested Authors
The Chocolate War (Robert Cormier)	Eight Plus One Other Bells for Us to Ring Tunes for Bears to Dance To Beyond the Chocolate War	Susan Cooper Jack London Gary Paulsen Richard Peck
Dealing with Dragons (Patricia Wrede)		
The Education of Little Tree (Forest Carter)	Watch for Me on the Mountain	
Face on the Milk Carton (Caroline Cooney)	I Am the Cheese The Bumblebee Flies Away Don't Look Behind You	Robert Cormier Lois Duncan Joan Lowrey Nixon
Face on the Milk Carton (Caroline Cooney)		
The Giver (Lois Lowry)	Eva Healer	Peter Dickinson
Hatchet (Gary Paulsen)	Call of the Wild Cookcamp Tiltawhirl John White Fang	Jack London
I Know What You Did Last Summer (Lois Duncan)	All titles/holdings of the authors	Joan Lowrey Nixon Christopher Pike R.L. Stine
Jeremy Thatcher, Dragon Hatcher (Bruce Coville)	Elmer and the Dragon My Father's Dragon The Dragonling Beware of the Dragon The Reluctant Dragon Eddie's Blue Winged Dragon	

TABLE III: (continued)

Patron Title	Suggested Titles	Suggested Authors
Lyddie (Katherine Paterson)	*Number the Stars*	
Motown and Didi: A Love Story (Walter Dean Myers)	*Waiting to Exhale*	
No Easy Place To Be (Steve Corbin)	*Their Eyes Are Watching God* *Mama* *Family*	James Baldwin Langston Hughes Zora Neale Hurston Alice Walker
Number the Stars (Lois Lowry)	*The Eagle Has Landed* *The Diary of Anne Frank* *Colony*	Jack Higgins Eugenia Price Anne Rivers Siddons
The Pelican Brief (John Grisham)		
Raney (Clyde Edgerton)	*Float Plane Notebooks* *Killer Diller* *In Memory of Junior* *Walking Across Egypt*	
Shattered (Dean R. Koontz)		
Sign of the Beaver (Elizabeth George Speare)		
Survivor (Gary Paulsen)		
Tune For Bears to Dance To (Robert Cormier)	*The Chocolate War*	

ians. Responses to the beginning question posed by the patrons were varied as in Phase I.

"I am going to refer you to someone else" led the patron to the reference librarian who admitted some vague familiarity with the book, Lois Lowry's *The Giver,* in one case. When the patron affirmed the librarian's speculation that this was a young adult title, she responded with a question, "What did you like about it that makes you want to keep reading?" The patron's indication of genre preference led the librarian to recommend an author of that genre. Once titles by the author were identified, the librarian concluded the dialogue with, "Look at these and let me know if I am on the right track." A noteworthy aspect of this transaction was that this closure provided an opportunity for the patron to return for additional assistance if needed. Also, the librarian probed with an inquiry about the book's appeal. No assumptions were made. Instead, the patron guided the interview and the librarian facilitated it as is expected in the most desirable strategy in readers' advisory work.

Another transaction began with the librarian's response of "What type of book is it?" This response to inquiry seems reasonable in early probing but the follow-through left the transaction unresolved for the patron.

> The librarian frowned slightly when she asked me what type of book it was that I had requested. She popped gum silently after I told her that it was a young adult book; then she turned around to the left and came out from behind the desk in a circle to me. She led me towards a section with a sign above it reading, "Easy Books" and stopped by a set of revolving stacks. Then she said, "All I can do is show you where we keep the kids' books. I don't know anything about young adult. We don't have that much."

She then left the patron and returned to the desk.

Comparing this case with the one previously cited, the title was confirmed as a title of young adult literature in both instances. Neither librarian knew much about pertinent titles, but in the first case, the librarian pursued the request by asking about appeal and in the second case, the librarian led the patron to the collection and left.

An approach revealed in most cases, in Phase II, which was also noted in the Phase I cases, is termed for purposes of this study "author assumption." In these instances, no consideration was given for the book's appeal except that of authorship. Librarians' search strategies focused on the mentioned authors' bodies of work and not much, if anything, else. When a patron asked about the *Chocolate War* by Robert Cormier, the response from the librarian was as follows:

> The first response was a look of bewilderment . . . quickly apologized for not being familiar with the title . . . asked me to tell her a little about the book to see if the summary would jog her memory . . . it failed . . . She asked if I simply wanted another book by the same author . . .

"Author assumption" need not be conclusive, but can also be an entry into focused probing. Initial response to Speare's *Sign of the Beaver* was "Try the catalog. Look for the author and see what else he's written." The librarian's candid response also revealed an unfamiliarity with the author, who is female. This transaction went no further.

The author was the first approach on the mind of another librarian in the case of *The Education of Little Tree*. And although some probing followed, it was not pursued, and the approach did not change to address the new information about appeal.

> OK. First, let's see what other books we have by the same author. Just a minute. [She was carding a book.] I think that used to be a biography, but they discovered it was fiction.
>
> She walked from behind the circulation desk to the OPAC. She asked a YA to move from the OPAC. He was just standing there, not using it. She typed in the titles to find the author and viewed sequentially the 6 volumes they had by Carter. I stood beside and watched. She mentioned that one title sounds interesting and could be found in the western collection. I asked, "Is *Education of Little Tree* considered a western?" She viewed that title and said, "No, regular fiction." She said, "I don't know what you liked about *Little Tree*. Did

you like it because it was an Indian story?" I responded, "Not really. I like the way it was written, very funny in parts—I laughed a lot; and sad, I cried a lot too." "Oh!", she said, "I haven't read it, but maybe I will. You can find these books in the fiction stacks or in the western collection." She pointed the way and I went to the stacks.

After being directed to the reference librarian, another patron in search of some advice on *The Pelican Brief*—an adult title of young adult appeal—was "directed to the online catalog to see if there were other books by this author. When I explained that this was not what I wanted, she directed me to the section for new books." The patron alerted the librarian that the direction of the transaction was not progressing satisfactorily, but to no avail as the librarian offered no further assistance.

One patron specifically asked for titles similar to those written by Clyde Edgerton, a North Carolina author of adult fiction. The patron wrote:

> . . . librarian supplied me with a list of Edgerton works and referred me to the information desk to find a "cross reference book" that tells other authors who write in the same style. [I had to ask for other authors.]

An admission of limited knowledge followed an attempt in "author assumption." Recognizing an author's title, a librarian recommended, "You might try *The Chocolate War*" when the patron indicated that she enjoyed Cromier's *Tunes for Bears To Dance To.*

> Librarian stayed behind the desk. When I indicated that *The Chocolate War* was not on the shelf as I had already looked, the only suggestion received was to browse in the Young Adult section. She admitted she had little knowledge of young adult literature.

Another case of assumption by a staff member on a subject heading remained very focused once it was discovered. "I enjoyed reading *Jeremy Thatcher, Dragon Hatcher . . .*" brought the response, "Do you know the author?" The patron confirmed Bruce Coville and the librarian checked the catalog for other books by the author. The subject heading, "Dragons," led to recommendations of other books about dragons—all by different authors.

The librarian respondent in another case asked the patron about the premise of the book because "she was not familiar with the author or the book."

> To her question, I described *Motown and Didi* as a love story involving two African American teenagers and their struggles to make life better for themselves, in spite of the drugs, death, and other evils they must face. At this point, she suggested that I browse through some of the other titles by Walter Dean Myers, and pointed in the direction where I might find them.

The description of plot by the patron in this case provided ample opportunity for the librarian to explore patron preferences, but instead, the focus remained on the author.

Somewhat different is the assumption of reader interest in the same genre as the book initiating the inquiry, leading to recommendations of other authors writing in that same genre.

> "I liked Lois Duncan's *I Know What You Did Last Summer.* What else can you suggest like that?" She named an author, Nixon, couldn't think of her first name and then moved over to the catalog where she found Jean Lowrey Nixon. She then tried to think of more authors and named Christopher Pike and R.L. Stine. She said they were scary and suspenseful but not too scary . . . She entered both authors' names and waited while the titles appeared . . . I thanked her.

The librarian moved from author- to genre-based on assumption only; no questions were asked of the patron.

A second case followed the same pattern.

> I approached the librarian in the young adult/children's

section and told her that I had just finished reading *Hatchet* and could she recommend something similar for me to read next. She pointed to the Young Adult fiction section while telling me that there were numerous stories by Paulsen that were similar to *Hatchet*. Before I could get to the section, she walked over to it and handed me [a Paulsen title] . . . She pointed out other adventure, survival stories that were grouped together by genre.

Again, although accurate in matching the genres—moving to Paulsen who writes adventure stories—to others in the genre, an assumption was made by the librarian that the patron wanted to remain in the genre. Options not explored could have been geographic setting or characterization, for example.

A case that involved "author assumption" and consultation of staff resulted in questionable final recommendations. The initial response to *Number the Stars* was "I'm not familiar with that book. Gee, I don't know. What's it about? I'm drawing a blank. I'm not sure."

The circulation desk worker was very nonchalant at first. She asked me twice who the author was. She asked, "Was the book a mystery?" She asked, "Was it the plot—time setting that you liked?" Then we walked to the stacks and she mentioned two other similar titles. She then mentioned a new book that had been ordered but had not yet arrived. At this point, she became agitated. She nervously searched for the librarian whom she could not find. She then pointed out Anne Rivers Siddons' *Colony* which she was very exuberant about. She loves this author and although it was completely different from what I was looking for, she felt that the characterization followed suit with my book. Finally, she located the librarian and questioned her expertise in this matter. The librarian readily acknowledged me and recalled the author of my book. "That's in the children's department," she said in surprise. However, she could not offer any suggestions in this area. When her cohort offered the *Colony* suggestion once again, stating that this book was nothing like my book except in characterization, the librarian agreed that I should try this book. I finally agreed to give it a try. During checkout, the circulation worker added, "If you don't like it, bring it back and we'll try something else."

The librarian's personal reading preferences prevailed in this situation even after learning that the patron's title was children's literature. Rivers is clearly an adult fiction author, most prominent in horror fiction.

Having become alert to cases of "ethnic elicitation," this researcher noted one case in Phase II that differed slightly from the earlier case. In the previously described *Motown and Didi* . . . title, eventually the librarian recommended *Waiting to Exhale* by African American author Terry McMillan, which is unequivocally an adult title, portraying adult situations, and probably most familiar to the librarian because of its best seller status. The recommendation could have been made on the basis of the ethnic perspective, which was related by the patron when describing the plot, but no confirmation was sought by the librarian.

Probing in this, which confirmed the appeal of Corbin's *No Easy Place To Be*, led to a satisfactory experience for the patron. The story chronicles the lives of an African-American family during the Harlem Renaissance. The patron reported:

> He was not familiar with the author at first. After telling him some background on the author, he was then able to help me . . . Since the book is centered around the Harlem Renaissance, he suggested other books that dealt with this period of history.

In this example, the librarian took full advantage of hints about appeal supplied in the description of the plot and was able to recommend appropriate titles.

Continuing discussion of examples of best practice leads us to Katherine Paterson's *Lyddie*. The librarian responded, "Do you want to read more books by Katherine Paterson?" The patron replied, "Not necessarily," and the librarian continued with, "Do you want historical novels?" In this case, the probing focused on identifying a genre and also revealed that the librarian was knowledgeable about children's and young adult literature as *Lyddie* is historical fiction. Also important to note is that the librarian did not assume that the patron wanted to read the author's works, but instead asked the patron if this was her preference. As the interview progressed, the librarian's expertise and competence in readers' advisory became more evident.

> I answered, "Yes, historical novels. Perhaps something with a strong female character." The librarian got up from the desk and walked to the reference section and got the book, *Gender Positive: A Teacher's and Librarian's Guide to Non-Stereotypical Children's Literature, K-8*. She opened it to the table of contents and pointed out that it was arranged by grade level and genre. I looked through it and copied down information. The librarian returned to her desk. I returned the book to her and thanked her, telling her that I had found some titles. She asked if I had read *Number the Stars*. She said it was hard to find many books right on the mark for a particular age level. She said *Lyddie* was a sixth to seventh grade book, and *Number the Stars* was more appropriate for fourth to fifth grade.

The suggested title can be classified as historical fiction. This case also involved consultation of a published source—one chosen specifically for the patron's needs as determined in the probing.

The same title, *Face on the Milk Carton*, was requested by two patrons. Both librarians began their roles in the transactions with "author assumption," but then diverted and later became part of a contrast study of worst and best practices.

In the first case, the patron was asked, "Do you want books by that author or books with a similar theme?" There was potential here for probing since the librarian asked instead of assumed an interest in theme or author. But, when the patron responded that "either would be fine," the librarian chose to pursue the author.

> She stated that she was not an expert in young adult fiction but that she would try to help. She turned to the online

catalog and punched in the author's name . . . When the information came up and showed all books by that author were checked out, she expressed surprise that the author was so popular. She did not pursue the subject approach or attempt to instruct me in the use of the online catalog. She stayed at her desk the entire time with no other people waiting to speak to her. To end the inquiry, she pointed in the general direction of young adult fiction and invited me to browse.

In the other case, the first response was, "That book is in our young adult section. Our professional in that area is busy . . . but let's see if I can get you started . . . We have several of the titles by that author. Let's go over to the shelves and take a look." Although perhaps in an unexpected order, the probing did occur.

> We browsed YA collection for other Cooney titles. Librarian said, "I haven't read that book, but I've read about it. What was it that you liked about the book?" I told her that I liked the three-dimensional characters and the emotional struggle of the main character. She saw the children's services librarian return to the desk and encouraged me to browse while she went to get the other librarian. I could overhear her telling the children's librarian what I was looking for. She was very thorough and accurate in reporting what I said.
>
> I was favorably impressed that a librarian in a different area would move to the children's desk when she saw a patron waiting. She made good eye contact with me and listened well. Even when she turned aside to check the OPAC, it was clear that she wasn't turning away from me. She spoke directly to me, not to the terminal.
>
> The children's librarian came over to me quickly and was able to help right away. She demonstrated real enthusiasm for YA literature and shared some of her personal favorites with me. She stopped when she saw that my arms were full. I came home with six books!

Obviously, this case contrasts sharply with the other in that, most importantly, the patron was very much satisfied. Also, there was follow-through in the probing and consultation with staff, both significant factors in successful readers' advisory practice.

An examination of these Phase II cases reveals a continuing trend of "author assumption" in which most librarians who admittedly were unfamiliar with children's and young adult literature sought to satisfy the patrons' requests with recommendations of the same author. In a few cases, the librarians who were most often reference librarians consulted colleagues who were children's librarians. There are about four librarians in the state of North Carolina who are considered full-time young adult librarians, so the fact that young adult librarians were not consulted was no surprise. Often, the practice is that children's librarians can provide the young adult services that are offered by a library.

In the absence of a librarian to consult, the staff member receiving the request usually did not consult any reference materials, but instead relied on the library's holdings as shown in the card catalog for OPAC. Most patrons were generally satisfied with their readers' advisory experiences in spite of these inadequacies.

General Observations and Conclusions

Only a few of the cases presented revealed a thorough approach to readers' advisory in children's and young adult services. For purposes of this discussion, an approach characteristic of best practices is one that seeks first to determine the patron's preference based on appeal, and second to focus on recommending appropriate titles based on that appeal. The determination is confirmed through probing that seeks to recognize exactly what aspect(s) of the book the patron finds appealing. Options include literary elements—setting (geographical and/or chronological), character type, author's style, theme—genre, and author's body of work. When follow-through to focus on the specific appeal does not occur, the success of the transaction becomes questionable. Professionals should exhaust all options and resources of consultation. These elements contribute to approaches of what are considered to be the best practice.

In the worst practice, librarians make decisions about the patron's preferences and thus compromise the integrity of the transaction. As these cases related above illustrate, two pitfalls are common—"ethnic elicitation" and "author assumption." When these two approaches undergird and drive the entire transaction, the patron is likely to be disappointed and shortchanged. However, if the respondent's inquiries based on ethnic perspective or author identity are used to begin probing, then they are legitimate as approaches to begin searches.

Another consideration is that most staff who may be consulted about children's and young adult literature are not likely to be familiar with—or comfortable in—advising someone about these bodies of literature. Nonetheless, if other librarians are unavailable, then a mechanism must be in place to assist the staff members, often not a librarian, to ensure delivery of the best service. Bibliographic sources are reasonable aids. Two rather current titles which were not available when student patrons collected data for this study, are invaluable resources. Library staff involved in readers' advisory services for children and young adults should use Pam Spencer's *What Do Young Adults Read Next: A Readers' Guide to Fiction for Young Adults* and Candy Colburn's *What Do Children Read Next: A Readers' Guide to Fiction for Children* both published in 1994 by Gale.

Connecting the reader and the text in a meaningful and satisfactory way is the professional obligation that should be embraced by all library staff. To ensure that the best service is rendered to the patrons, research designed to ascertain best practices should continue, for there is a dearth of research in this area. This report of research is an early contribution to this new knowledge base of research in readers' advisory services for children and young adults.

Notes

1. Rosenblatt, L.M. "The Literary Transaction: Evocation and Response." *Theory Into Practice* 21 (1982): 271.

2. Applebee, A.N. *The Child's Concept of a Story.* Chicago: University of Chicago Press, 1978. p. 124.

3. ———. Op. Cit. pp. 123–125.

4. Beach, R. and L. Wendler. "Developmental Differences in Response to a Story." *Research in the Teaching of English* (1987): 295.

5. Karetzky, S, *Reading Research and Librarianship: A History and Analysis.* Westport, CT.: Greenwood Press, 1982. p. 3.

6. ———, Op. Cit. p. 19.

7. Chelton, M.K. "Educational and Recreational Services of the Public Library for Young Adults." *Library Quarterly* 48 (1982):488.

8. Jones, P. *Connecting Young Adults and Libraries.* New York: Neal-Schuman Publishers, 1992. pp. 80–81.

9. Lundin, A. "The Company We Keep: Advisory Service for Youth." *Developing Readers' Advisory Services: Concepts and Commitments.* (McCook, K. and G. Rolstad, G., eds.) New York: Neal-Schuman Publishers, 1993. p. 45.

10. United States Department of Education. *Services and Resources for Children in Public Libraries.* Washington, D.C.: Office of Educational Research and Improvement. p. 8.

11. United States' Department of Education. *Services and Resources for Young Adults in Public Libraries,* 1988. p. 10.

Chapter Three:
One Reader Reading: A Case Study

by Duncan Smith

> I find that the largest group, two sevenths of the whole, read
> mainly to kill time. About one fifth read around their voca-
> tion, one seventh around a possible new vocation or an avo-
> cation. One-seventh offer evidence of a serious purpose to
> rise to a higher cultural level; rather more than a seventh hop
> about from vocational to cultural, from good to bad.[1]

$\mathcal{M}$y opening quote represents one path that is frequently taken by
individuals who are trying to develop a clearer understanding of readers and reading. It is taken from Alvin Johnson's *The Public Library—
A People's University*. Mr. Johnson's evidence for his quote is his
examination of the reading records of 1,000 patrons of the Newark
Public Library for a six-month period during the late 1930s. Johnson
was attempting to clarify for himself and librarianship the ways in
which the public library could be a full partner in the adult education
movement of that time. His thesis was that the public library, through
its staff, could have a positive impact on its users. Though he offers
no direct evidence of a librarian guiding the reading of the patrons he
studies, he assumes this influence is present and that it is a positive
one. In his concluding pages Johnson makes the following statements:

> Yet one thing is reasonably clear to anyone who patiently
> goes through record after record of library experience. Where

the records exhibit a high degree of rational development, someone, probably a modest library assistant who would deny any active intervention, has given advice.[2]

Johnson offers no concrete evidence for this statement. It is a statement that probably derives its validity from something that Kathleen De La Pena McCook has dubbed the "Library Faith."[3] As has already been pointed out elsewhere in this book, Sharon Baker feels that unsubstantiated statements like these may be one of the reasons for the decline in readers' advisory service in public libraries in the United States.[4] There is also an implication in Johnson's statement that systematic reading is evidence of an external source of guidance. He does not seem to entertain the notion that orderly or systematic reading may be the result of a reader responding to needs, urges and knowledge that orginate from within herself.

Johnson may have inherited this point of view from both the professional culture and the societial milieu which was operant in the 1930s and 1940s. Another example of his culture's influence on his investigation is in the way in which he sought to investigate this entire issue. First of all, he examined patrons' reading records, not patrons' reading experiences. Secondly, he frequently assumes that the readers of his day and the ones to follow are able to examine a list of books and immediately understand what the reader's motiviations were in reading them and in fact whether the reader was rising to a higher cultural level or merely killing time. In one passage, Johnson offers six pages of the reading record of a housewife. The pages consist of the date, the author, and title of the books checked out by the reader. Based solely on this information, Johnson says, "And finally, who can note without sympathy this record of a housewife's literary adventure."[5]

Johnson's book was published in 1938 by the American Association for Adult Education. In the same year, Louise M. Rosenblatt published *Literature as Exploration*. Rosenblatt, a college English teacher, offers a very different view of readers and reading. She places her emphasis not on the text but the reader. The following quote from Rosenblatt's preface to the third edition of her work gives a flavor of her stance toward reader, text, and reading:

The reader counts for at least as much as the book or poem itself; he reponds to some of its aspects and not others; he finds it refreshing and stimulating, or barren and unrewarding. Literature is thus for him a medium of exploration. Through books, the reader may explore his own nature, become aware of potentialities for thought and feeling within himself, acquire clearer perspective, develop aims and a sense of direction. He may explore the outer world, other personalities, other ways of life. Liberated from the insularity of time and space, he may range through the wide gamut of social and temperamental alternatives that men have created or imagined. Part of my task will be to outline some of the realms into which the reader may thus penetrate, and to sketch some of the personal and social benefits that may flow from such literary discovery.[6]

While both Johnson and Rosenblatt are discussing the reading experience, their visions of that experience quickly diverge from each other. Johnson chooses to focus on the book or text while Rosenblatt chooses to focus on the reader's evocation of the text. When librarianship came to this fork in the road, the majority of librarians chose to follow Johnson and focus on the text. Each generation of librarians stands at the same fork in the road and each generation must choose which path it will take. It is my hope as we stand at this fork in the road, that some of us will choose the path that Rosenblatt took and writes about. I have been exploring that path for four years now and I feel that for me—it has made all the difference.

Accompany me a little ways down this path, the path that Rosenblatt speaks so elegantly about. But before I begin an examination of specific readers and their experiences, I would like to acknowledge some colleagues who have taken the path less traveled ahead of me.

Trailblazers

Rosenblatt is one of many educators who have sought to develop a deeper understanding of the literary experience through the analysis

of their students' responses to literature. Rosenblatt pays homage to
I.A. Richards. Richards' *Practical Crticism* is an analysis of the response of his undergraduate students to poetry.[7] Published in 1929,
Richards' work exerted a profound influence on the work of Rosenblatt. Other examples of studies of this sort include the work of James
R. Squire, Norman Holland, and Patricia Enciso-Edmistein. Squire
studied the responses of fifty-two ninth and tenth graders to four
short stories.[8] Norman Holland combined the results of psychological
tests with in-depth interviews to develop individual portraits of how
five undergraduates experienced Faulkner's "A Rose for Miss Emily."[9]
Patricia Enciso-Edmistein utilized several strategies such as reading
logs, classroom observation, in-depth interviews, and reenactments of
significant passages to examine how five middle school students experience both assigned texts and texts they read for themselves.[10] These
are a few of the examples of the many published and emerging studies
in the field of education that focus on the student's experience of literature. Studies of this type yield a wealth of information about how
readers read. For the advisor of adult readers, however, their value is
limited by the fact that their subjects are usually in a school or other
academic institution and they are usually under twenty-one years of
age. Most readers' advisors in public libraries are dealing with users
who are choosing texts for their own reasons and not reading texts
that someone else has pre-selected.

In part due to the renaissance in popular culture studies, several
individuals have begun to study the reading habits and preferences of
the adult general reader. Janice Radway's *Reading the Romance:
Women, Patriarchy, and Popular Literature* is an excellent example of
this genre.[11] In *Reading the Romance*, Radway conducts an ethno-
graphic study of a group of Midwestern women who read romance
novels. Her study consists of in-depth interviews, a survey of reading
interests and habits and an analysis of the romance texts these women
viewed as "ideal" and of those the women viewed as "failed." What
emerges from Radway's work is a complex portrait of the ways in
which a particular group of readers read, how reading fits into their
lives, their reading behaviors, and their values in terms of what a
"good" book is and what it is not. One of her findings was the fact
that the readers in her study tended to read a book's ending first.

Radway's readers did this because a "good" book had a happy ending. Since these readers had to fit their reading into a very busy schedule, they did not want to invest their time, money, and selves in a book that would not satisfy them.

A student of Radway's, Erin Smith, has begun similar research on women who read mysteries. Smith is interested in exploring why women read mysteries that have female detectives as the protagonist. As part of her research, Ms. Smith asked members of a local Sisters in Crime chapter to complete a survey instrument. She also conducted in-depth interviews with several members of this chapter. Sisters in Crime is an organization that was originally founded to assist and support women mystery authors. One of Smith's early findings was that the women in her study tended to focus more on the character of the female detective than the plot of the novels they read. Her subjects could provide her with a wide range of information about their favorite female detectives, but frequently could not recount the plot of specific novels in which their favorite character appeared. Smith also found that readers were frequently attracted to a particular author, character, or novel because of the novel's setting. For example, one of her readers stated that one of the reasons she liked to read Robert Parker's Spenser series was because the series is set in Boston and Cambridge. The reader used to live in this area and felt that Parker was very good at describing this locale.[12]

A Danish librarian who has made a significant contribution to this area is Annelise Mark Pejtersen. As part of her attempt to develop a classification scheme for fiction, Pejtersen analyzed conversations conducted between librarians and patrons. These conversations were readers' advisory transactions. What emerged from this analysis were basic parameters for what people talk about when they talk about books. Pejtersen found that readers frequently discussed the subject content of the novel; the novel's setting in time and place; the theme of the novel; i.e., the author's attittude towards the subject or the ideas and emotions which the author wants to communicate to his readers; and finally the level of communication or readability of the book.[13]

Another librarian who has made a contribution in this area is Catherine Sheldrick Ross.[14] Ross used open-ended interviews to investigate the reading interests and experiences of adult general readers in Canada. Ross provides a thorough review of the readers' advisory literature. Her discussion of how browsers ask themselves questions about new authors and titles they encounter is particularly interesting. She cites Pejtersen as a example of someone who has conducted in-depth investigations in this area. She also found that readers tended to derive a wide range of benefits from a wide range of texts. Ross's work expands and elaborates on the earlier work of the Sabines in their publication *Books That Made The Difference.*[15] In their work, the Sabines asked individuals to respond to the questions "What book made the greatest difference in your life?" and "What was that difference?" One of the conclusions of the Sabines' work was that a wide variety of books influence readers. Because of the detailed nature of her instrument, Ross not only confirms this finding but provides a much more detailed account of how readers are affected by the reading they themselves choose. Her article contains a rich tapestry of readers and their experiences, which every readers' advisor should read.

The boundaries for developing a map of a reader's experience begins to emerge from these studies. The borders of that map would consist of some combination of the following: characater, plot or genre, setting—either time or place or both—the theme or subject of the story, and some elements of the reader's affective experience of the story itself. Using these factors we can begin to develop an understanding of a specific reader's experience of a specific text. These factors are only the beginning. They serve as the frame for what is frequently a very complex picture. In order to develop a complete picture of readers and reading, we need to provide them with an opportunity to develop. Readers' advisory service is about providing this opportunity. With that in mind, I would like to provide you with an opportunity to view some readers and their reading.

A Gallery of Readers

The ultimate objective of readers' advisory services is to increase a reader's access to authors and titles that meet their needs. In order to be effective readers' advisors, librarians must attempt to understand what reading means to a specific reader and what aspects of a book contribute to that reader's enjoyment. This means that librarians must shift their focus, which has traditionally been on reference sources and the contents of books to the reader, the reader's experience and the advisor's understanding of that experience.[16]

The most effective means of gathering information about a reader's experience is through the use of open-ended questions. In *Readers' Advisory Service in the Public Library*, Joyce Saricks provides readers advisors with an excellent open-ended question: "Tell me about a book you really enjoyed."[17] This question and questions like it allow a reader to describe their experience rather than require them to analyze it. What follows is a series of portraits of readers as they respond to my version of the Sarick's question, which is "Tell me about a book you've read and enjoyed." Each of the following portraits are transcripts from videotaped responses to this question.

One of the challenges for readers' advisors is to really listen to a patron's response to "Tell me about a book you've read and enjoyed." This task is more difficult than it seems because each of us has a view of readers and reading that is based on our experience. There is a great temptation to view the way each of us reads as the only way to read and to view individuals who chose to read different texts from the ones we chose or readers who employ different reading strategies from ours as inferior. For example, because I read to discover what will happen to the characters I am reading about, I viewed the reading of a book's ending first as an abomination. This action makes perfect sense, however, for Radway's readers, and upon hearing her explanation for this behavior, I learned to value this strategy as an effective reading strategy for those readers with needs similar to Radway's readers. By really listening to reader's responses to open-ended questions, a readers' advisor can develop a fuller understanding of the wide variety of readers and reading that occur in their communities.

Here is one individual's response to "Tell me about a book you've read and enjoyed." This reader is a white female with advanced college degrees. She is a participant in a book discussion group that has been meeting for several years.

I'd like to tell you about *Absalom! Absalom!* by William Faulkner. The reason I liked that book, well there were a couple of reasons. I liked the fact that a story is revealed through the course of the novel. It is a story within a story and there is a constant retelling of the same story and with each retelling more facts of the story are revealed. So that by the end of the novel you know all the facts of the story.

I liked it because there is a depth of narration and description. I liked the really dense description. I liked the character development. I'm not sure what else I liked about it.

I guess I liked the writing. It was a pleasure to read the writing. I thought it was very well written. Although others complain about William Faulkner, I like the dense description. I guess that is as much as I can tell you about what I liked in the book and what I generally like in novels and literature.

While this reader does not discuss the characters, plot, setting or theme of *Absalom! Absalom!*, there is something familar about this reader's discussion of her reading. Her focus on language and technique and her focus on the author is comforting for those of us who were English majors in college. This patron belongs to the taste culture that Herbert Gans refers to as "high-culture."[18] Individuals who belong to the high culture taste group pay particular attention to the construction of cultural products. In this case, notice the reader's attention to "dense description" and the "pleasure" of reading the writing. Another aspect of the "high-culture" perspective is its emphasis on character over plot. Subtlety is another. Notice again this reader's explicit statement about character development. Also her statements about the story being revealed indicate an interest in the subtle way in which Faulkner weaves and reweaves his tale.

This reader is discussing a text which is in the "canon." The "canon" is that English major approved list of titles that all educated individuals "should" read. This reader's response is not the only way in which one can respond to a text that is in the "canon." In fact, Robert Coles in his work The *Call of Stories: Teaching and the Moral Imagination* discusses how some of his students react to works of literature and the deeply personal connections that occur for some of them. Coles' students are frequently individuals who are professionals or who are taking college courses for fun or individuals who had to delay their college experiences for a variety of reasons. He tells of a lawyer who goes to the public library to read rather than repeat his father's use of alcohol to deal with the moral dilemas his work sometimes presents and a young doctor who is concerned that he will wind up being a "society doc" like Dr. Lydgate in Eliot's *Middlemarch.* Coles reminds us that sometimes a character, setting, or situation encountered in our reading can reasonate with our own experience and create a moment of recognition and reflection about ourselves and our lives. He states that some of his students "have learned to regard the characters in novels as persisting voices."[19] This finding compares with Erin Smith's that women who read mysteries that have female detectives as their protagonists frequently talk about these characters as though they were real people. The readers in Smith's study frequently referred to these characters as people who kept them company or in metaphors that would be used for a companion.[20]

As Smith's work with women mystery readers shows, the ability to become attached to a particular character or a situation in a novel is not restricted to texts that are in the "canon." In fact, texts which have not received favorable critical attention and even texts about which a particular reader is skeptical can have a powerful and lingering affect. Take for example, this reader's experience with Robert James Waller's *The Bridges of Madison County.* The reader is a white female who is also a public librarian.

> The book I have really enjoyed the most in the last couple of months is *The Bridges of Madison County.* It was a surprise to me because I've heard patrons talking about it and I thought "Oh, it sounds like a little mushy love story" and I don't know that that is anything I'd be interested in. But because it stayed on the *New York Times'* Bestseller list for so long and because so many people were talking about it, I decided that I needed to read it for myself.
>
> So a couple of weeks ago, I checked it out and I went home and read it overnight. It's not a very long novel. It was interesting because I thought about it and I'm still thinking about it weeks later. In terms of what it made me think about

in relationship to my own life and the fact that it was a simple story on the surface.

There wasn't any figuring out to do with it other than the thought processes it triggered in me in terms of figuring out my own life and where I am. I think it spoke to me mostly because I just turned forty-one and I'm in the process of thinking about the roads I've taken and the roads I haven't taken over the course of the last twenty years or so. And decisions I've made and why I've chosen certain things.

This book was about a woman who fell in love with a photographer who just happened to be travelling through this midwestern town filming bridges—covered bridges. And it was an immediate physical attraction and their affair lasted three or four days while her husband and children were at the state fair. She spent the rest of her life looking at the letters— not letters but the pictures and a letter he had sent her. She had decided that she couldn't go off with this guy because of her responsibilites to her husband and her children.

And I think about the fact that at the age of twenty, I would have gone. I wouldn't have hesitated, I would have jumped in that truck and been gone with this guy. And now I don't know that I would make that decision. So anyway, its triggered just an enormous amount of thinking on my part in terms of my own life and it's a beautiful story.

Each of these readers demonstrates one way of reading. To use Rosenblatt's phrase, they are examples of a reader's evocation of a text. They can also serve as guideposts for our use in doing readers' advisory work; however, each reader is an individual whose reading preferences and evocations is the result of a wide variety of factors as the next section of this article will show.

A Life Story

I have known Elizabeth* as a colleague for about ten years. She graduated from the library school where I have been employed as a

---

*In the interest of privacy, name has been changed.

continuing education coordinator and an enrollment manager. Elizabeth has served on several of the planning committees I have used to plan continuing education events. She served on the planning committee for the Popular Literature conference, which has been mentioned elsewhere in this book. Elizabeth was one of the first individuals I videotaped as part of my readers' advisory workshop.

Three years ago, I moved into Elizabeth's neighborhood. Our neighborhood is a cul de sac that consists of sixteen upper-middle-class homes. All of the homes were built by a female-owned construction company. One of the owners is Elizabeth's partner for life. Both Elizabeth and her partner have been dinner guests in my home. We frequently see each other at afternoon barbecues and deck parties. Libraries, books, reading, and readers are a major topic of conversation between us. Our conversations frequently draw comments like "Here they go again," from our friends and neighbors. Elizabeth is a devoted walker and it is not usual for me to see her and her dog either beginning or returning from their walk as I leave for work in the morning. Her home and her garden are in plain view. Elizabeth is a passionate gardener. She faithfully tends it and its development has been one of her most prized creative acts. We share an interest in antique roses and she often brings books about this subject to my attention. We also share an interest in cooking. As a result of this shared interest, cookbooks, recipes, and tastes of new dishes flow back and forth between our homes.

Because of her interest and her accessibility, I decided it might be interesting to tape Elizabeth periodically responding to "Tell me about a book you've read and enjoyed." I thought it might be interesting to look for trends and to see if her tastes and interests remained constant over time. Because she was also responding to several suggested titles, I could also track her fiction selections over time. At this point, I have three videotapes in which Elizabeth responds to "Tell me about a book you've read and enjoyed." These tapes were made at various times during 1991, 1993, and 1994. The 1993 tape also contains Elizabeth's reactions to five titles suggested by me. In addition to these tapes, Elizabeth has provided me with the following documents and evidence relating to herself, her reading, and her reading interests. At my request, she wrote a brief autobiographical sketch. This sketch focused on several of her life's significant moments. Elizabeth has also kept a reading journal for the past three years. This journal contains brief annotations and comments on all of the books she has read from 1990 through early 1994.

Using this material, it is possible to track Elizabeth's path through contemporary literature in much the same way a biographer tracks the development and growth of his subject. But before I begin to re-construct Elizabeth the Reader, I want to examine the condensed ver-sion of this woman's life story.

My first significant moment happened when I was in elemen-tary school. I was on a field trip with the Georgia Mineral So-ciety, and instead of finding the crystal we were looking for, I found a perfect arrowhead. A professor from Emory Univer-sity was on the trip, and as I greatly admired Emory, I ran up to him and showed him my treasure. He was nice and told me of the probable tribe. Warming up, I told him I wanted to be an archeologist when I grew up. He looked down his pipe stem and said "The last thing the world needs is another woman archeologist!" I was crushed.

My second significant memory of a significant "event" was my high school graduation. I was one of the speakers and had several awards (State DAR History, top female all-round student, top social studies student, outstanding senior, editor of the paper, assistant editor of the yearbook, etc.). I had achieved my goal of getting a full scholarship to college, but except for that tangible fact, it all seemed rather empty. I had "done it all" (in a very small, working class/poor high school)—big fish in a very shallow, small pond, but it was not particularly satisfying. I think this revelation changed how I approached college and my life. I would attempt at least to live it on my terms and not other people's. This was very clear to me that day. I can remember the scene as well as the feel-ing.

The third event happened in college. In 1968, I was a Southern Baptist Summer Missionary in an experimental program that paired me with a young woman from the National Baptist Convention. The National Baptist Convention is an organization of black Baptists. We lived with a black family in Kansas City, Missouri working in inner-city churches. Two things changed in me from this experience. I learned about poverty, and how it is color blind, and how many poor people work much harder than I ever would. And I learned what it was like to be in the minority. Some weeks I lived in a completely black world: churches, stores, swimming pools, restaurants. This whole summer was the most difficult and most expanding of my life. I never told my parents that I was working and living with black people.

Returning to college, I knew things would be different. I needed to stay in Georgia and teach in exchange for my scholarship. But I wanted something more than a suburban Atlanta school. With an eclectic group from school, I visited Koinonia Farms outside of Americus, Georgia. Koinonia, founded in 1941, is an community with a mission of pacifism, interracial justice and economic justice. (This is in rural southwest Georgia, mind you.) Our group listened to tapes by founder Clarence Jordan (who had died the year before) and was given a tour by the two "partners" who had visitor's duty. One was a Hutterite doing his CO (conscientious objector); the other was a New York native who had burned his draft card. I thought both were a bit strange. But I had made the belief of racial justice my own, and felt the War (as we called the Vietnam War) was wrong, and as I read the New Testament, a good case could be made for economic justice being part of life for anyone trying to be a Christian. So I moved to this strange place, where I was the only white Georgian, based only on what they believed. It was one of the best decisions of my life. While folks laughed at the way I talked in my own state; I found wonderful people who became family to me, Koinonia-"fellowship" in the true sense of that word. Living at that place, at that time, profoundly changed the way I looked at myself, my faith, and the world. This was the fourth and most significant event in my life.

While at Koinonia, a group of women began meeting,

and talking about our roles, in the community, in relationships, and in the Bible. During the spring of 1974, I attended a conference in Atlanta of Women in Campus Ministry. (I went with a campus minister who was living at the farm for a semester.) There the fifth major event happened. A real feminist clique. Being with women in the ministry, hearing their struggles with sexism and faith, was earth-shaking for me. I knew I had to see for myself if Christianity and feminism were possible. For this, I felt I must leave my true home, a most painful experience, but I knew beyond a shadow of a doubt this was the right thing for me to do.

I looked at schools in Boston, but decided to move to Durham to attend Duke Divinity School. I helped start the Lucrecia Mott Feminist Caucus at the Divinity School and had a great time with the other six or seven women in my class. While most of the women in that class stayed in some form of ministry, I was moving more and more to the belief that the basic tenets of the Christian faith were sexist and women would never be more than second class citizens in such a masculine/male-based faith. I symbolically flunked "Conversion and Nurture," a class that was gradeless! The professors were not happy to comply with my symbolic act of leaving the church!

While at Duke, my best friend from Koinonia moved to Durham; we became lovers and "came out" as lesbians. We were together for three years, in the very heady early political lesbian community of the Triangle. These were the years of the "Personal being Political"—a saying I still like.

My last significant event was meeting my partner for life at a gathering of women—lesbians and straight—that happened as a happy hour every Thursday at a downtown Durham restaurant. (She always likes to remind me it was in the bar of the restaurant!) We have become a family, own a home, and try to live in a just and loving way to each other and the world.

Three themes emerge from this autobiographical narrative. These themes are the quest for a personal identity, the search for community, and the establishment of a personal religious and political presence in the world. Elizabeth's search for and struggle to establish her identity is introduced in the first scene of her story. She experiences firsthand the male world's narrow view of what is possible for women when the male professor from Emory belittles her desire to be an archeologist. Elizabeth's search for a personal identity plays itself out in the next scene, when she experiences the emptiness of having succeeded on terms other than ones own. These experiences combine to lead her to explore and experience the world in broader terms than "suburban Atlanta" and lead her to her experiences in Kansas City, Koinonia, Duke Divinity School, and finally her home with her found family in Durham. The second theme running through Elizabeth's story is her search for community. This search is introduced in the section of her narrative which discusses her experiences in Kansas City. In this section, she feels what it is like to be a minority and in her case to be in a community but not part of it. This eventually leads her to Koinonia, where she encounters people whom she felt at first were a "bit strange." She eventually moves to this "strange place, where I was the only white Georgian" and where "folks laughed at the way I talked in my own state." This sense of being "physically" at home (i.e., in Georgia) eventually yields to being "spiritually" at home as Koinonia becomes a place where strange people become wonderful people and family. At Koinonia, Elizabeth encounters the fellowship of women. This becomes a major theme for her and the remainder of her narrative focuses on her deepening relationships with women and eventually her partnering with a woman. At the same time, the third major theme of Elizabeth's narrative is reintroduced. Elizabeth's commitment to the establishment of a personal religious and political presence in the world is introduced in the Kansas City section of her story. It is elaborated on during her residence at Koinonia. It becomes personal, however, during her tenure at Duke's Divinity School with her symbolic flunking of a "gradeless" course and her involvement in the women's and lesbian communities in Durham. Her quoted slogan "Personal being Political" is an appropriate anthem for this portion of her life. Elizabeth's narrative ends in a summary of her quest and its outcomes "We have become a family, own a home, and try to live in a just and loving way to each other and the world."

This narrative was written during March, 1994. My first videotaping of Elizabeth occurred in 1991. Elizabeth's first response to "Tell me about a book you've read and enjoyed" appears below:

> I really liked the book *The Prince of Tides* by Pat Conroy. I was really surprised that I liked it because about 80 percent of the books I read are by women and I am skeptical also about people who write about the South because I'm a Southerner and I often feel that when people write about the South, they distort it. This book was recommended to me by a friend and I reluctantly finally read it and when I did, I couldn't put it down. It was like I couldn't eat, I couldn't sleep, I just had to read this book.
>
> It's about, to use today's lingo, a dysfunctional family, and it's dysfunctional beyond anything you could imagine. There's two brothers and a sister and a mother and a father and some grandparents who are just basically crazy. And its very, very funny; very, very, beautiful; and very, very tragic all at the same time. It's just this strange mix of people and events set in the marshes that I just love.

A comparison of these two narrative passages reveals certain connections—some obvious, some which will emerge when other examples of Elizabeth's reading are examined. Most apparent is her statement about 80 percent of the books she reads being authored by women. This certainly is in keeping with her continued exploration of her own identity as a woman and her relationships with women. In terms of *The Prince of Tides* itself, Elizabeth spends a great deal of time discussing how she came to this book and its effect on her. When she does talk about the "story" itself she focuses on the family and the dynamics of the family "which is basically crazy." Family and the meaning of family is a theme that appears in several of the scenes in Elizabeth's life story. One can also hear echoes of her first encounter with the "strange" individuals doing "visitor's duty" at Koinonia. Her experience of *The Prince of Tides* is not unlike her experience of Koinonia. The dysfunctional family of *The Prince of Tides* dissolves into a story that is very, very funny; beautiful; and tragic. This process in some ways mirrors the way in which Koinonia ceases to be a strange place with strange people and becomes a place of wonderful people, fellowship, and family. The tragic moment for Elizabeth occurs when she must leave this place of fellowship and family to continue her development as a person.

There is also the case of Tom Wingo, the hero of *The Prince of Tides*. In a way his story is reminiscent of Elizabeth's high school accomplishments. Tom finds himself empty at mid-life. When we meet Tom, his career is ruined, his marriage is ending, and his family is "basically crazy." Like Elizabeth, Tom leaves the marshes he loves and goes into a strange environment (i.e., New York City), where to his amazement he rediscovers himself and returns home to reestablish both himself and his family.

The importance of place in both Elizabeth's life and its importance in her story world is indicated in two ways in her description of her experience with *The Prince of Tides*. The importance of place to Elizabeth is indicated by her concern about books written about the South being distorted. She is concerned that the "place" of the South will be misrepresented and therefore will form a barrier to her ability to enter the world of the story. She also indicates the importance of place with her concluding statement "set in the marshes that I just love." It is interesting to note that *The Prince of Tides* opens with Tom Wingo's statements, "My wound is geography. It is also my anchorage, my port of call."[21]

The role that place plays as a means for Elizabeth to enter and derive satisfaction from a story world is elaborated on in her second response to "Tell me about a book that you've read and enjoyed." This second response was recorded during 1993.

The book I've enjoyed the most recently is *Bootlegger's Daughter* by Margaret Maron. This is an author that lives in Garner (NC). It's a mystery featuring Deborah Knott, who's a woman attorney running for a district judge seat, and she is also trying to solve a twenty-year-old murder. What takes this book from a genre to a book of substance is the incredible setting and feel it has for North Carolina. At one point, when she's bumfuzzled, she goes looking for arrowheads in a ploughed field and the description of that was very evocative for me. The mystery is a tight mystery. It has some political overtones. The women characters are very strong and the men characters are real and believable and also good. She has friends in Raleigh and they talk about coming to the Triangle, and I can't tell you any more about it because it's a mystery and it would spoil the book. But it's just about one of the best mysteries I've read in the last couple of years and I highly recommend it for anyone who likes mysteries or books about North Carolina.

The most striking thing about this transcript is the connection that exists betweeen it and Elizabeth's autobiographical sketch. Even though they are separated by a period of approximately eighteen months, scenes involving arrowheads appear in both. I feel that one of the reasons Elizabeth finds Maron's book so evocative is the similarities that exist between the story world of *Bootlegger's Daughter* and the primary world of her life. The presence of an arrowhead in both is only one of several similarities. In her autobiography, Elizabeth discusses the importance of women to her and her own political activities. Maron's heroine is involved in a political race; she is running for a judge seat. Elizabeth opens her discussion of Conroy's *The Prince of Tides* by stating that 80 percent of the books she reads are by women. The importance of setting to Elizabeth was also mentioned in her discussion of *The Prince of Tides*. It is interesting to note that when Elizabeth elevates *Bootlegger's Daughter* to "a book of substance" the criterion that is used is Maron's ability to evoke a sense of place. Another connection between the story world of *Bootlegger's Daughter* and Elizabeth's primary world is that the part of North Carolina Maron so successfully evokes is the part of North Carolina in which Elizabeth lives.

Each of these episodes, the scenes from Elizabeth's life, and her reactions to two books she read and enjoyed contribute to a portrait of Elizabeth's reading tastes. So far it appears that she likes books by and about women, books in which a sense of place is evoked, and books which are either mainstream fiction or mysteries. In order to further clarify which of these values were primary and which were secondary, I did two things. First of all, I took a reader type on Elizabeth. The concept of reader type was developed by Robert Thomas in his book *Toward An Aesthetics of Junk Fiction*.[22] In this book Thomas argues that within each genre there are several categories of readers. Each category exists in each genre and all readers have some relationship with each genre. Thomas says that for any given genre, a reader is either an exclusivist, a regular reader, a sometimes reader, an infrequent reader, an allergic, or a fan. I identified Elizabeth's type for each of the following genres: western, mystery, romance, science-fiction, fantasy, horror, mainstream, historical and adventure. This determination was made through a series of directive questions. I would start the series by saying something similar to the following: "I am going to ask you a few questions about various genres and whether or not you read them. For example, do you read westerns?"

In Elizabeth's case, her response to this question was never. For westerns, Elizabeth was classified as an allergic. In some cases, additional clarifying questions were used to make a final determination. In the adventure genre, Elizabeth indicated that she had read some adventure stories but not many. Clarifying questions were needed in order to determine whether she was a sometimes or infrequent reader in the adventure genre. As a result of this process, I discovered that Elizabeth was a regular reader of science fiction and fantasy. She was also a fan of these genres. Elizabeth was a sometimes reader in the mystery, horror, mainstream and historical genres. She was allergic to the western and romance genres. Because Elizabeth reads so widely, genre is a useful indictator of her reading preferences but not one that can be used in isolation in identifiying her reading tastes.

The second thing I did in order to further clarify Elizabeth's reading tastes was to seek her reaction to five titles I suggested. A review was provided for each of the titles. Elizabeth was provided with a "booklist." I allowed her a few minutes to examine it and then I videotaped her reaction. The booklist appears below[23]:

Corpi, Lucha. *Eulogy for a Brown Angel.*
Corpi (*Delia's Song*—not reviewed) brings a Chicana feminist perspective to the mystery genre and does with originality to overcome some stilted and murky writing. The story begins

when civil-rights activist Gloria Damasco discovers the body of a murdered child on an L.A. street during a Chicano demonstration in 1970. Damasco has a "dark gift," an uncontrollable extrasensory awareness that's stirred by this discovery and that will bring her back to investigate it time and again until the truth is finally revealed in 1988. When a gang member who may know the killer's identity is also murdered, Damasco works with a dying police detective to reveal a second killer, but that effort apparently closes all doors to the mastermind behind the killings. She eventually returns to her family in Oakland, believing the crime will never be solved, although she keeps collecting information about the case over the years. Many readers will have pinpointed the killer's identity long before the heroine does, but one last nasty secret is revealed in the bloody conclusion that adds an extra wallop to the convoluted goings-on. (*Kirkus* Reviews, reprinted with permission)

Hess, Joan. *Maggody in Manhattan.*

Arly Hanks, Police Chief of Maggody, Arkansas, is forced out of her sleepy everyday routine after Ruby Bee, her diner-owner mom, wins a trip to New York as a finalist in the Krazy Koko-Nut cooking contest. Ruby's frantic call from jail brings Arly to New York's Chadwick Hotel, ostensibly in the process of renovation, where the finalists are staying. Turns out that Durmond Pilverman, another contestant, was found naked and slightly injured in Ruby's bed, and Ruby was arrested and briefly held in the ensuing commotion. But that's just a start to the jumble of goings-on at the Chadwick—as a body turns up in the dumpster outside; another is found in the raunchy club where contestant Gaylene dances; teen-aged contestant Catherine seems to be a drunken nymphomaniac; cartons of Krazy Koko-Nut are laced with cocaine; and the mob is running the hotel. Woven through all this is Arly's hot affair with Durmond—plus scandalous news from home. (*Kirkus* Reviews, reprinted with permission)

Kelly, Susan. *Out of the Darkness.*

Cambridge freelancer Liz Conners (*And Soon I'll Come to Kill You*, etc.)—now helping handsome, mega-selling true-crime author Griffin Marcus research his book on the serial killing of seven (or is it nine?) Catholic women found slashed on the banks of the Merrimack—soon finds herself doubting his premise: that they were slaughtered by Henry Kmiec, imprisoned for another, unsuccessful attempt. While wrestling with her detective lover Jack Lingemann's chauvinism, and with Marcus' put-downs of her murder reconstructions, Liz and the cop-sister of a victim turn up new evidence—then the sister is killed, Kmiec becomes a suicide in his cell, and another victim (same M.O.—multiple stab wounds in the chest and neck and a jaunty green bow tied above them) is found by the Merrimack. Now separated from Jack and romancing Marcus, Liz must confront several more deaths before the grisly, if none-too-believable, resolution. . . . (*Kirkus* Reviews, reprinted with permission)

Malone, Michael. *Time's Witness.*

The text of the review Elizabeth reacted to is on p. 412 of *Fiction Catalog*, 12th Edition, New York: The H.W. Wilson Company, 1991.

Taylor, Elizabeth Atwood. *The Northwest Murders.*

In a third outing, P.I. Maggie Elliott (*The Cable Car Murder, Murder at Vassar*) recovering from a debilitating illness, is living in northern California, in the remote forest cabin left to her partner Richard O'Reagan by his Aunt Bessie. Its peaceful ambiance is shattered by news of the gruesome killing of a young hiker and the rape of his girl companion, who's comatose in a nearby hospital. Maggie, to her horror, discovers that the girl is Sally, daughter of her old friend Hallie Stephens. Sally will be at risk as long as the killer is loose, and Maggie promises her mother that she'll try to find the culprit. The lonely mountain-trail site of the murder has a surprising number of frequenters—little Hermina, an Indian girl whose

great-grandmother's cabin is due to be razed by the Forest
Service; a Chinese man staying in a motel who claims to be
just a tourist; gossipy old-timer Joey Brown; Bill Dawson,
looking for signs of Bigfoot; and several others. By the time
Maggie succeeds in getting a wrongly accused Indian off the
hook and brings the real villain into the open, there will have
been more murders and a further attempt on Sally's life.
(*Kirkus* Reviews, reprinted with permission)

These five titles were selected to provide me with more information about Elizabeth's reading tastes. Based on her discussion of her
reactions to *The Prince of Tides, Bootlegger's Daughter,* and her
reponse to my questions about her interest in various genres, I knew
that she liked books by women, that an evocative setting was an important factor in her enjoyment of a book and that she was a regular
reader of several genres. In an attempt to further identify which of
these factors might be more important, I decided to test whether the
gender of the author and protagonist or the setting was more important. In order to test this, the booklist I provided her contained five
mysteries. Four of these were by women and had female protagonists.
One was by a man and had a male protagonist.

Here is a transcript of Elizabeth's video-taped reaction to these
titles:

Of these books, and I'm not familiar with this author, the one
I'd probably read first is *The Northwest Murders*. I like the
idea of the wilderness. I like the connection between the P.I.
whose doing the investigation, it was one of her friend's
daughters. I like the Native American flavor. That sounds really good.

I've read Joan Hess and I like her so I'd probably read her
next. Just because I'm familiar with that author. I like the idea
of her having to go with her mother to a cooking contest that
seems sort of interesting and the murder sounds interesting
in a raunchy club. That sounds like an interesting affair—
place for a murder.

I'd probably read *Eulogy for a Brown Angel*. This particular review says that the writing is murky and I don't like that. But the idea of a Chicana feminist detective I like a lot. It sounds interesting that the detective has a little ESP. I think that might be fun.

Out of Darkness, I'm not familiar with this author—it sounds interesting—a serial killer. I don't usually like serial killer ones, so maybe I wouldn't read this one next.

But I probably would because even though I've got a lot of friends who really liked *Time's Witness*. An enlightened redneck police chief does not grab me right off the bat. So that would be the order I'd read them in.

Given a list of titles in which genre is totally controlled and the gender of both author and main character is controlled in four of five titles, Elizabeth appears to use setting as the factor that determines her reading choices. Setting is viewed as more important even when she has read and enjoyed one of the authors on the list. Even though Elizabeth has enjoyed Joan Hess' work, the setting in *The Northwest Murders* is the first factor she gives for making it her first choice. She also comments on the personal connection between the P.I. and one of the victims, who is the daughter of an old female friend. All of the other titles written by women and that have female protagonists were chosen over Michael Malone's book. These titles are preferred even though in one case, the writing is murky and in another case the "serial killer" theme is not one that is usually enjoyed.

The role of gender and setting is also evident in Elizabeth's reading journal. Here are a few sample entries:

Star Trek: The Pandora Principle by Carolyn Clowes
04-26-90
Good Trek story—with Kirk in a vault and Mr. Spock the captain of the Enterprise with his half Vulcan and half Romulan protege who is a woman—good story, good character.

Coyote Waits by Tony Hillerman
07-09-90
One of the best with Jim Chee and Joe Leaphorn. Good fe-

male character, lots of lore—good mystery. Didn't guess it. Looking for the body of Butch Cassidy.

Bedrock by Lisa Alther
07-13-90
About on the level of Kinflicks. Two women artists, married, who love each other but don't become lovers because of their families or art. Some funny lines—some nice views of country illusions v. realities and art. But not up to *Other Women* or my favorite, *Original Sins.*

Track of the Cat by Nevada Barr
06-16-93
Great mystery in high country of Guadalupe Mountains in west Texas—a national park. Rangers are getting killed in "accidents" and Ranger Anna Pigeon thinks something is up. Panthers are released and disappear. Ranchers hate the park. Great stuff on National Park Service. Anna almost falls in love with a woman who is a lesbian.

These few entries cannot take the place of a comprehensive analysis of Elizabeth's reading journal. But as they show, the themes of women characters and setting continue to play a major role in Elizabeth's reading life.

I recently videotaped Elizabeth for a third time. This tape was made during the spring of 1994. I would like to close this article by providing you with an opportunity to examine this last tape for yourself and allow you to draw your own conclusions about Elizabeth and her reading interests:

The book that I'm reading right now that I'm really enjoying is *The Rising of the Moon* by Flynn Connelly. It's a futuristic book taking place after the year 2000 and a woman who had to leave Ireland to teach Irish history has come back to find out that the State has been taken over by the Catholic Church, by the radical right of the Catholic Church. And she's trying to find other women and men who are wanting a freer society.

There's a side plot that the rest of the countries have been contacted by the Unity. Which is a group of aliens who will give space flight to the countries of the Earth if they would stop fighting. The Irish and the other fundamentalist states which are the United States and a couple of Moslem countries have blocked all information about this. So this is a real neat little subplot that is going on.

And as the main character—I can't pronounce her name because its some Celtic goddess, even though its not some mythological kind of thing. She travels around Ireland meeting small cells of other women and men. The men happen to be the remnants of the Irish Republican Army which lost out when Ireland was unified in the year 2000.

And it's just fascinating because it talks a lot about family and religion and about women's place in society. And it's also a pretty good adventure story and also has the conflict between when is violence OK and when is violence not OK. And it's a real good crossover between science fiction and sort of like history—sort of like a futuristic history book.

Notes

1. Johnson, Alvin. *The Public Library—A People's University* (New York: American Association for Adult Education, 1938), p. 19.

2. Johnson, *The Public Library*, p. 20.

3. De La Pena McCook, Kathleen. "The First Virtual Library," *American Libraries* 24 (July/August 1993): 626.

4. Baker, Sharon L. "Readers' Advisory Services: A Call for More Reseach," *RQ* 32 (Winter 1992): 166–169.

5. Johnson, *The Public Library*, p. 13.

6. Rosenblatt, Louise. *Literature As Exploration*, third edition (New York: Noble & Noble, 1976): p. v.

7. Richards, I. A. *Practical Criticism: A Study of Literary Judgment* (New York: Harcourt, Brace, and Company, 1950).

8. Squire, James R. *The Responses of Adolescents While Reading Four Short Stories* (Champaign, IL: National Council of Teachers of English, 1964).

9. Holland, Norman. *5 Readers Reading* (New Haven, CT: Yale University Press, 1975).

10. Enciso-Edmistein, Patricia. "The Nature of Engagement in Reading: Profiles of Three Fifth Graders' Engagement Strategies and Stances" (Ph.D. dissertation, Ohio State University, 1990).

11. Radway, Janice A. *Reading the Romance: Women, Patriarchy, and Popular Literature* (Chapel Hill, NC: The University of North Carolina Press, 1984).

12. Smith, Erin. "Women and Contemporary Detective Fiction" (unpublished paper):30.

13. Pejtersen, Annelise Mark. "Fiction Retrieval: Experimental Design and Evaluation of a Search System Based on Users' Value Criteria," *Part 1, Journal of Documentation* 39 (December 1983): 230-46; *Part 2,* 40 (March 1984): 25-35.

14. Ross, Catherine Sheldrick. "Readers' Advisory Service: New Directions," *RQ* 30 (Summer 1991): 503-518.

15. Sabine, Gordon and Patricia Sabine. *Books That Made the Difference* (Hamden, CT: Shoe String Press, 1983).

16. Smith, Duncan. "Reconstructing the Reader: Educating Readers' Advisors," In *Developing Readers' Advisory Services: Concepts and Commitments,* edited by Kathleen de la Pena McCook and Gary O. Rolstad (New York: Neal-Schuman Publishers, 1993), pp. 21–29.

17. Saricks, Joyce G. and Nancy Brown. *Readers' Advisory Service in the Public Library* (Chicago, IL: American Library Association, 1989), p. 33.

18. Gans, Herbert. *Popular Culture and High Culture: An Analysis and Evaluation of Taste* (New York: Basic Books, 1974), pp. 75–81.

19. Coles, Robert. *The Call of Stories: Stories and the Moral Imagination* (New York: Houghton Mifflin, 1989).

20. Smith, Erin. "Detective Fiction," p. 26.

21. Conroy, Pat. *The Prince of Tides* (New York: Houghton Mifflin, 1986), p. 1.

22. Roberts, Thomas J. *Toward An Aesthetics of Junk Fiction* (Athens, GA: University of Georgia Press, 1990), pp. 71–86.

23. The titles listed were reviewed in the following periodicals and sources. Lucha Corpi—*Eulogy for a Brown Angel* (*Kirkus* July 1, 1992: 815); Joan Hess—*Maggody in Manhattan* (*Kirkus* July 15, 1992: 883); Susan Kelly—*Out of the Darkness* (*Kirkus* July 15, 1992: 884); Michael Malone—*Time's Witness* (*Fiction Catalog* 12th edition, New York: H.W. Wilson, 1991, p. 412); *Elizabeth Atwood Taylor—The Northwest Murders* (*Kirkus* July 15, 1992: 886).

Chapter Four:
Readers' Advisory in Public Libraries:
An Overview of Current Practice

by Robert Burgin

$\mathcal{E}$ven though readers' advisory represents an important service for public and school libraries, little is known about its practice. The processes followed by most librarians in trying to help patrons find fiction titles of interest are largely unknown, and the decision to employ a particular technique may often be based on little more than experience or anecdotal evidence. There is little empirical evidence regarding the extent to which various practices are employed or the relative effectiveness of these practices. As Baker recently pointed out in her outline of a research agenda in this area: "To date, little research has verified the extent to which [various readers' advisory] techniques have been adopted by libraries."[1]

Nevertheless, an understanding of these practices would be important in helping librarians better meet the needs of a large number of their patrons. A recent study by Shearer notes that 77 percent of all public libraries saw one of their principal roles as providing popular materials to their patrons, and fiction regularly represents a large percentage of the total materials circulated by public libraries.[2]

The research that has been done in readers' advisory has focused on specific techniques for making patrons aware of authors and titles of interest. For example, Baker has examined the effectiveness of fiction classification as a way to help library patrons find appropriate materials.[3] But aside from Baker's work, Harrell's study of the ways in which librarians classify adult fiction appears to be the only example of published research that examines the use of specific readers' advisory techniques in libraries.[4]

More is known about the nature and practice of reference transactions in libraries, and the research that has been conducted in this area may serve as a model for research in readers' advisory. Of particular interest are studies of the effectiveness of various techniques in providing reference services.[5]

Methodology

The study reported in this paper examined various aspects of the current practice of readers advisory in public libraries. A nine-question survey instrument (see the appendix at the end of this chapter) was mailed to the nearly 200 librarians who attended a September 1993 conference on readers' advisory. Of these, 111 completed questionnaires were returned. The instrument was also pretested with a group of fifty-one librarians who attended smaller readers' advisory workshops in 1992 and 1993, and these completed forms were included in the analysis for a total of 162 questionnaires.

In addition to demographic information (educational level, professional degree status, experience), the instrument gathered data on the frequency of readers' advisory transactions, the reading habits of the librarians themselves, and the likelihood that the librarians would consult certain sources or engage in certain actions in providing readers' advisory service. In essence, the study is an attempt to answer Baker's call for research to determine "the extent to which various readers' advisory techniques are being used."[6]

It is important to note that the individuals surveyed do not represent a random sample from the population of all public librarians or even all public librarians involved in readers' advisory work. The individuals attending the workshops were obviously interested in the topic and motivated to improve their skills in this area, perhaps more so than the typical public librarian doing readers' advisory. The extent to which the findings reported below may be generalized, then, is somewhat limited. Nevertheless, given the dearth of information in

Table 1: General Characteristics of Respondents		
Education		
High school graduate	5	(3%)
Some college	19	(12%)
College graduate	31	(19%)
Post college	107	(66%)
M.L.S. degree?		
No	85	(53%)
Yes	77	(48%)
Public library experience		
Less than one year	8	(5%)
One to four years	29	(18%)
Five to nine years	43	(27%)
Ten or more years	82	(51%)
Frequency of readers' advisory questions		
Five or more times a day	36	(22%)
At least once a day	71	(44%)
At least once a week	34	(21%)
Less than once a week	20	(12%)

this area, any empirical findings represent an important step towards gaining an understanding of current practice in readers advisory services.

Findings—General Characteristics

The survey instrument collected data on educational level, degree status, public library experience, and frequency of readers' advisory questions for each respondent. General characteristics of the respondents are shown in Table 1.

Nearly two-thirds of those surveyed (66 percent) had some post-college education; over four-fifths (85 percent) were college graduates. As might be expected, the majority of respondents with post-college education (77 of 107, or 72 percent) had the M.L.S. degree, but interestingly, thirty of the respondents had post-college education in other fields. Almost half of all respondents (48 percent) had the M.L.S. degree.

Over half the respondents (51 percent) had ten or more years experience in public libraries, and over three-fourths (77 percent) had at least five years' experience. Those with the M.L.S. degree tended to have more experience than did those without the M.L.S.: 87 percent of the professional librarians surveyed had five or more years of experience in public libraries, while only 68 percent of the paraprofessional librarians surveyed reported that level of experience.

The questionnaire asked respondents to indicate how frequently they received readers' advisory questions from patrons. Almost half the respondents (44 percent) reported receiving readers' advisory questions at least once a day. Two-thirds of the respondents (67 percent) reported receiving such questions at least once a day or more frequently.

Table 2: Reading Preferences and Characteristics of Respondents		
Genres Read		
General fiction	156	(96%)
Mystery	138	(85%)
Romance	95	(59%)
Other	79	(49%)
Science Fiction	57	(35%)
Fantasy	51	(32%)
Horror	45	(28%)
Western	29	(18%)
Fiction titles read		
50 or more per year	58	(36%)
12–49 per year	85	(53%)
Fewer than 12 per year	18	(11%)
Listed titles read (of nine)		
None	34	(21%)
One	37	(23%)
Two	24	(15%)
Three	31	(19%)
Four	27	(17%)
Five	7	(4%)
Six	1	(1%)
Seven	1	(1%)

Findings—Reading Preferences and Characteristics

Respondents were asked three questions regarding their own reading. The reading preferences and characteristics of the respondents are shown in Table 2.

The questionnaire asked respondents to list the genres in which they read the equivalent of at least one book per year. The most frequently listed genres were general fiction, reported by almost all of the respondents (96 percent) and mysteries, reported by over four-fifths of the respondents (85 percent). Of the remaining genres, only romances were reported by more than half of those surveyed; 59 percent reported that they read at least one romance title per year. Westerns represented the least frequently listed genre, with only one respondent in six (18 percent) reading that genre. Fewer than half the respondents reported reading at least one title in these other genres: horror (28 percent), fantasy (32 percent), and science fiction (35 percent).

Respondents were also asked to indicate the number of fiction titles read per year, and the majority of those surveyed (53 percent) reported reading from twelve to forty-nine fiction titles annually. Over one-third (36 percent) reported reading fifty or more fiction titles per year, and only one in nine (11 percent) read fewer than twelve fiction titles annually.

The survey instrument used in this study was developed for use in a series of readers' advisory workshops that included tapes of library patrons discussing books that they had recently read and enjoyed. Titles mentioned by these patrons were listed on the survey instrument, and respondents were asked to indicate which of the titles they had read. Random sampling techniques were not used in the selection of patrons for taping nor in the selection or titles listed; nevertheless, the titles represent those read by individuals who are not atypical of the patrons encountered in public libraries.

As might be expected, some of the titles had been read by a large number of respondents and some had not. The most often read titles were Pat Conroy's *The Prince of Tides* (read by 61 percent of the respondents), Mary Higgins Clark's *All Around the Town* (41 percent), and Amy Tan's *The Joy Luck Club* (41 percent). The titles that were read least often were *The Journey of the Soul,* a Muslim tale by Abu Bakr Muhammad bin Tufail (read by none of the respondents), Guy Kay's *Tigana* (2 percent), and Guy Kay's *The Fionavar Tapestry* (2 percent). Interestingly, the latter two titles are fantasies and therefore represent a genre that was less often read by the respondents. The ma-

Table 3: Resources and Actions Identified by Respondents		
Most frequently used resource		
Personal reading	36	(35%)
Readers' advisory sources	18	(18%)
Patron comments	17	(17%)
Other	11	(11%)
Booklists, bookmarks, etc.	8	(8%)
Reviews	7	(7%)
Book jackets	5	(5%)
Reading of family or friends	1	(1%)
Reading of colleagues	0	(0%)
Actions taken in readers' advisory		
Consult sources that would help identify authors and titles	119	(84%)
Recommend based on personal knowledge	118	(83%)
Ask a colleague for help in identifying authors and titles	111	(78%)
Direct the patron to the appropriate shelving area	91	(64%)
Provide the patron with a bookmark, booklist, etc.	82	(58%)
Instruct the patron in the use of these sources	79	(56%)
Other	22	(16%)

jority of those surveyed (59 percent) had read two of the listed titles or fewer, but over one third (37 percent) had read four or more.

Findings—Resources and Actions

Respondents were also asked questions about their use of resources in making suggestions to patrons about additional authors or titles and about the actions that would likely be performed in a readers' advisory situation. These findings are summarized in Table 3.

The survey instrument asked respondents to list the one resource most frequently used in making suggestions to patrons about additional authors or titles. The results discussed here are based on the replies of the 103 respondents who listed only one resource. (The replies of thirty-seven respondents who listed more than one resource have not been included in the analysis. Another twenty respondents from the pretest attended a workshop at which this section of the survey instrument was omitted.)

The most frequently listed resource was personal reading, selected by 35 percent of the respondents. Readers' advisory sources (18 percent) and patron comments (17 percent) were the next most frequently selected sources. By contrast, none of the respondents listed the reading of colleagues as the most frequently used resource, and other infrequently listed resources included the reading of family and friends (1 percent), book jacket information (5 percent), reviews (7 percent), and booklists, bookmarks, or other printed matter (8 percent).

It is important to note the specific wording of the question in interpreting the findings outlined above. Respondents were asked to select the one resource most frequently used in making suggestions to patrons about additional authors or titles. Had the question allowed respondents to list all resources that might be used, the percentage of respondents listing resources such as book jacket information and reviews might have been higher. It is interesting, for instance, to note that of the thirty-seven respondents who incorrectly chose more than one resource, personal reading was still the most frequently listed resource (87 percent) while book jacket information (43 percent) was listed least frequently.

Finally, the survey instrument asked each respondent to list the actions that would be taken if a patron came to the library and requested readers' advisory assistance. Here, in contrast to the previous question, respondents were asked to check as many actions as they felt appropriate. Because twenty respondents from the pretest attended a workshop at which this section of the survey instrument was omitted, the results outlined here are based on only 142 respondents.

Three actions were listed by more than three-fourths of the respondents. Consulting sources to help identify authors or titles that the patron might enjoy was listed by 84 percent of those surveyed, followed by making recommendations based on personal knowledge (83 percent), and asking a colleague for help (78 percent). Even though other actions were less frequently listed, all actions were listed by at least half the respondents; the least often chosen actions included instructing the patron to use sources to help identify authors or titles that the patron might enjoy (56 percent); providing the patron with a bookmark, booklist, or other printed matter (58 percent), and directing the patron to the appropriate shelving area (64 percent). One in five respondents listed five actions (22 percent), while another one-fourth listed four actions (26 percent).

Further analysis of the responses indicates that the use of resources and the actions performed in the readers' advisory situation were affected by certain characteristics of the respondents' reading. For example, heavy readers listed personal reading as the most frequently used resource significantly more often than did those who read fewer fiction titles in a year. Nearly half of the respondents who read 50 or more titles per year (48.7 percent) chose personal reading as the most frequently used resource; by contrast, only 29 percent of those who read from twelve to forty-nine titles per year and none of those who read fewer than twelve titles per year listed that as the top resource (Chi-square=8.435; df=2; p=.015).

This finding is confirmed by a similar relationship showing that heavy readers were more likely to give recommendations based on personal knowledge than were those who read fewer fiction titles. Nearly all of the respondents who reported reading fifty or more titles per year (98 percent) listed making recommendations based on personal knowledge as an action that would be taken in a readers' advisory situation. By contrast, only 82 percent of those reading from twelve to forty-nine titles per year and fewer than half of those reading fewer than twelve titles per year (47 percent) selected this action (Chi-square=23.218; df=2; p=.000).

Similar relationships were also found between reliance on personal knowledge and the number of listed titles read, which could be seen as another gauge of the amount of fiction read by a respondent. For respondents who listed personal reading as the most frequently used resource, the mean number of listed titles read was 2.86; for respondents who did not select personal reading, the mean number was significantly lower, only 1.82 (t=-3.224; df=101; p=.002). Likewise, for those respondents who listed making recommendations based on personal knowledge as an action that would be taken in a readers' advisory situation, the mean number of listed titles read (2.22) was significantly higher than the mean number of titles read by respondents who did not select that action (1.50) (t=1.989; df=140; p=.049).

Another reading characteristic, the number of genres for which a respondent read at least one title per year, was also related to the reliance on personal knowledge. For respondents who listed making recommendations based on personal knowledge as an action that would be taken in a readers advisory situation, the mean number of genres in which they read at least one title per year (3.70) was significantly higher than the mean number of genres listed by respondents who did not select that action (2.63) (t=3.218; df=140; p=.002). Interestingly, the difference in mean genres listed was not significantly different for those who listed personal reading as the most frequently used resource (3.97) and those who did not (3.48).

Not only were those who listed personal reading as the most frequently used resource more likely to be heavier readers (as defined by the number of listed titles read), those who listed other resources as the ones most frequently used were less likely to be heavier readers. For example, for respondents who listed patron comments as the most frequently used resource, the mean number of listed titles read was only 1.35; for respondents who did not select patron comments, the mean number was a significantly higher 2.35 (t=2.350; df=101; p=.021). Likewise, for respondents who selected booklists, bookmarks, and other printed matter as the most frequently used resource, the mean number of listed titles read was only 0.88; for respondents who did not select that resource, the mean number of listed titles read was significantly higher (2.30) (t=2.419; df=101; p=.017).

One of these relationships also held for breadth of reading (as defined by the number of genres in which a respondent read at least one title per year). For respondents who listed patron comments as the most frequently used resource, the mean number of genres listed was only 2.77; for respondents who did not select patron comments, the mean number was a significantly higher 3.83 (t=2.629; df=101; p=.010).

Findings Related to M.L.S. Degree

Respondents were asked whether they had received an M.L.S. degree, and questionnaire results could be analyzed in order to determine whether professional librarians reported readers' advisory practices that differed from those reported by non-degreed, paraprofessional librarians.

Only three differences of statistical significance were found. Those with the M.L.S. reported receiving significantly fewer readers' advisory questions than did those without the degree; while 32 percent of the non-degreed librarians reported receiving five or more such questions a day, only 12 percent of the degreed librarians reported receiving questions this frequently. By contrast, respondents with the M.L.S. were twice as likely to report receiving readers' advisory questions less than once a week (see Table 4). This finding may reflect the fact that the professional librarians who attended the workshops and

Table 4: Frequency of Readers' Advisory Questions by M.L.S. Status				
	No M.L.S.		M.L.S.	
Five or more a day	27	(32%)	9	(12%)
At least once a day	37	(44%)	34	(45%)
At least once a week	14	(17%)	20	(26%)
Less than once a week	7	(8%)	13	(17%)
(Chi-square=11.518; df=3; p=0.009)				

thereby received the survey instruments tended to be in supervisory positions that took them "away from the desk," while those without the M.L.S. tended to be in "front-line" positions that allowed them more direct and more frequent interaction with patrons. The finding may also reflect the fact that many readers' advisory transactions take place at the circulation desk, which tends to be staffed by paraprofessionals, rather than at the reference desk, which tends to be staffed by professional librarians.

Respondents with the M.L.S. degree also tended to be heavier readers than did those without the degree. While the percentage of professional librarians who reported reading fifty or more fiction titles per year was somewhat higher than the percentage of parapro-fessional librarians who reported reading that many (40 percent v. 33 percent), the difference was not statistically significant. However, the professional librarians reported reading significantly more of the nine titles listed on the survey instrument. For respondents with the M.L.S. degree, the mean number of those titles read was 2.38; for respon-dents without the degree, the mean number was only 1.78 (t=2.410; df=160; p=.017). It is interesting to note that while the professional li-brarians tended to read more titles, they did not read in more genres. Both M.L.S. and non-M.L.S. respondents reported a mean of 3.5 genres in which they read at least one title per year. Reading heavily does not necessarily entail reading widely.

Finally, respondents with the M.L.S. degree were more likely to consult sources to help identify authors or titles that the patron might enjoy. While 91 percent of the professional librarians listed this action, only 77 percent of those without the degree did (Chi-square=4.833; df=1; p=.028). It is perhaps not surprising that those with the M.L.S. degree would feel more comfortable with and knowledgeable about such sources; one would expect that instruction in the use of such sources would be part of the library school curriculum.

Discussion

Two points should be noted here regarding the results of the sur-vey. First, none of the findings is particularly surprising. Respondents who were more comfortable relying on their personal knowledge in a readers' advisory transaction were likely to be those who read more and who read in a wide range of genres. By contrast, those who felt less comfortable with their personal knowledge and who therefore re-lied more on patron comments and booklists were likely to be those who read less or who read in fewer genres. Likewise, it is not surpris-ing that persons with the M.L.S. degree, who should have received some instruction in the use of readers' advisory sources in library school, would be more likely to consult those sources to help identify authors or titles that the patron might enjoy.

However, what is perhaps surprising is that more relationships were not found among the variables in this study. For example, what is noteworthy is not that the professional librarians were more likely to use resources in a readers' advisory transaction, but that they did not differ significantly in other ways from their colleagues without the degree. While it is heartening that persons with the M.L.S. degree were more likely to use those sources, it is not encouraging that they were not more likely to instruct patrons in the use of such sources, to ask colleagues for assistance, or to provide printed materials such as bookmarks and booklists.

Likewise, it is somewhat surprising that the resources used most frequently and the actions taken most often did not vary with years of experience and were not affected by the frequency with which a librarian receives readers' advisory questions. Neither those with more public library experience nor those who performed readers' advisory more often differed in their resources and actions from those with less experience and those who infrequently dealt with such questions. Instead, the variables that appeared most likely to affect a librarian's choice of resources and actions in the readers' advisory transaction were those related to that individual's reading habits and preferences. Those who read more and who read in more genres appeared to be more likely to rely on that personal knowledge.

Conclusion

The findings reported here represent an attempt to outline some characteristics of readers' advisory services in public libraries and some characteristics of the professional and paraprofessional librarians who provide those services. The respondents were not randomly selected but instead represented individuals who attended readers' advisory workshops and were perhaps more interested in the topic and more motivated than the typical public librarian doing readers' advisory to improve their skills in this area. Nevertheless, the findings do represent a first step towards understanding current practice in readers' advisory services.

Based on the respondents to the survey reported here, readers' advisory services were being provided primarily by college graduates who had worked in public libraries for at least five years. The librarians tended to receive at least one readers' advisory question daily and tended to read at least one fiction title per month, usually in general fiction and mysteries. When attempting to answer readers' advisory questions, those surveyed here relied most frequently on personal reading and were most likely to consult sources to help identify authors or titles that the patron might enjoy, make recommendations based on personal knowledge, and ask a colleague for help.

Among the respondents, the heavier readers were more likely to rely on personal reading as a resource and were more likely to give recommendations based on personal knowledge. By contrast, those who read less were more likely to rely on patron comments and booklists, bookmarks, and other printed materials. Those with the M.L.S. degree, while reporting fewer readers' advisory questions, tended to be heavier readers but also were more likely to consult sources to help identify authors or titles that the patron might enjoy.

While these findings contribute to our understanding of the readers' advisory process, it is also important to note that the present study has been restricted to trying to understand the processes followed by most librarians in trying to help patrons find fiction titles of interest. No attempt has been made here to gather empirical evidence regarding the relative effectiveness of these practices, and such studies are badly needed. As Baker notes: "A related research question is whether [readers' advisory] techniques are effective in increasing patron satisfaction with and use of the library . . . Unfortunately, the amount of such research is small, and there is almost no research on the extent to which direct help from a readers' advisor can increase patron satisfaction with or use of library resources".[7]

We know, for example, that personal reading was the most frequently listed resource and that heavier readers were more likely to rely on that personal reading, but we do not know whether it was an effective resource. We know that instructing the patron to use sources to help identify authors or titles that the patron might enjoy was the least frequently listed action, but we do not know whether it might be a more effective option than those more frequently selected. While we may speculate that the heavy reliance on personal reading shown by the respondents to this survey is unwise (especially in light of the fact that so few of the respondents read in genres like westerns, horror, fantasy, and science fiction), hard data are needed to show whether the use of personal reading as a resource is appropriate.

Obviously, more research in readers' advisory is needed. It is appalling that we know so little about a service that is so important to public and school libraries. While 77 percent of all public libraries saw a primary role as providing popular materials to their patrons, little is known about how readers' advisory services are provided or, perhaps more importantly, how they ought to be provided.[8]

Librarians have only recently begun to investigate the nature and practice of reference transactions, and the work being done in that area is exciting and important. It is hoped that a similar degree of attention will now be focused on readers' advisory and that equally exciting and important findings will result from that research.

Acknowledgment

This research was supported in part by a North Carolina Central University Faculty Research Grant.

Notes

1. Baker, Sharon L. "Readers' Advisory Services: A Call for More Research." *RQ* 32 (Winter, 1992): 167.

2. Shearer, Kenneth. "Confusing What is Most Wanted with What is Most Used: A Crisis in Public Library Priorities Today." *Public Libraries* 32 (1993): 193-197.

3. Sharon L. Baker, writing alone or with co-investigators has produced much along these lines: "Overload, Browsers, and Selections." *Library and Information Science Research* 8 (1986): 315-329; "Why Book Displays Increase Use: A Review of Causal Factors." *Public Libraries* 25 (1986): 63-65; "Fiction Classification Schemes: An Experiment to Increase Use." *Public Libraries* 26 (1987): 75-77; with Gay W. Shepherd "Fiction Classification Schemes: The Principles Behind Them and Their Success." *RQ* 27 (1987): 245-251; with Gay W. Shepherd as lead author "Fiction Classification: A Brief Review of the Research." *Public Libraries* 26 (1987): 31-32; and "Will Fiction Classification Schemes Increase Use?" *RQ* 28 (1988): 366-376.

4. Harrell, Gail. "The Classification and Organization of Adult Fiction in Large American Public Libraries." *Public Libraries* 24 (1985): 13-14.

5. Some interesting recent studies on reference transactions include: Durrance, Joan. "Reference Success: Does the 55 Percent Rule Tell the Whole

Story?" *Library Journal* 114 (1989): 31-36; Dyson, Lillie S. "Improving Reference Services: A Maryland Training Program Brings Positive Results." *Public Libraries* 31 (1992): 284-289; Hernon, Peter and Charles R. McClure. "Unobtrusive Reference Testing: The 55 Percent Rule." *Library Journal* 111 (1986): 37-41; and Stephan, Sandy, et. al. "Reference Breakthrough in Maryland." *Public Libraries* 27 (1988): 202-203.

6. Baker, Sharon L. "Readers' Advisory Services: A Call for More Research." *RQ* 32 (1992): 167.

7. Ibid.

8. Shearer, Kenneth. Op. Cit.

Appendix

Good Leads to Good Reads
Participant Demographics

Please respond to the questions listed below.

1. Check the highest level of education you obtained:
   - _____ Less than high school graduate
   - _____ High school graduate
   - _____ Some college
   - _____ College graduate
   - _____ Post college

2. Do you hold a master's degree in library science?   ____ Yes   ____ No

3. How many years of public library experience do you have?
   - _____ Less than one year
   - _____ One to four years
   - _____ Five to nine years
   - _____ Ten or more years

4. How often do you personally receive readers' advisory questions from patrons?
   - _____ Five or more times a day
   - _____ At least once a day
   - _____ At least once a week
   - _____ Less than once a week

5. Please check the genres in which you read the equivalent of at least one book per year. Check as many as apply.
   - _____ Fantasy
   - _____ General Fiction
   - _____ Horror
   - _____ Mystery
   - _____ Romance
   - _____ Science Fiction
   - _____ Western
   - _____ Other, please specify_____

6. How many works of fiction do you read?
   - _____ 50 or more per year
   - _____ 12–49 per year
   - _____ Fewer than 12 per year

7. Please check all of the books you have read from the list below:

_____ *Tigana* by Guy Kay
_____ *The Prince of Tides* by Pat Conroy
_____ *All Around the Town* by Mary Higgins Clark
_____ *Hondo* by Louis L'Amour
_____ *The Joy Luck Club* by Amy Tan
_____ *The Journey of the Soul* by Abu Bakr Muhammad bin Tufail
_____ *Kane and Able* by Jeffrey Archer
_____ *The Fionavar Tapestry* by Guy Kay
_____ *Bootlegger's Daughter* by Margaret Maron

8. Which of these resources do you use most frequently in making suggestions to patrons about additional authors and titles they might like to read? Check only one.

_____ My personal reading
_____ The reading of my family or friends
_____ The reading of my colleagues
_____ Patron comments
_____ Reviews
_____ Book jacket information
_____ Readers' advisory sources
_____ Booklists, bookmarks, or other printed matter that provides information on authors or titles
_____ Other, please specify_____

_____

9. In general, if a patron came into your library and requested assistance in locating additional adult fiction authors and titles, which of the actions listed below would you take? You should check as many as needed in order to provide an accurate picture of your usual response to a readers' advisory question.

_____ Make recommendations based on my personal knowledge without consulting sources.
_____ Direct the patron to the appropriate shelving area in the library.
_____ Consult sources that would help me identify authors or titles the patron might enjoy.
_____ Instruct this patron in the use of these sources.
_____ Ask a colleague for help in identifying authors and titles that might be of interest to the patron.
_____ Provide this patron with a bookmark, booklist, or other printed material that contained information about authors or titles the patron might enjoy.
_____ Other, please specify_____

_____

The following information is optional and will be kept confidential. Thank you.

Name _____

Public Library _____

Branch (if applicable) _____

Street address _____

City/State/Zip code _____

Chapter Five:
Librarians' Abilities to
Recognize Reading Tastes

by Duncan Smith

*I*n "Best Practices: An Analysis of the Best (and Worst) in Fifty-Two Public Library Reference Transactions" Catherine Sheldrick Ross and Patricia Dewdney provide a glimpse of public library reference transactions from the patron's point of view.[1] Their article is a sobering examination of what actually happens when a patron enters a public library and asks a question. Ross and Dewdney allow us to experience our user's satisfactions and disappointments. Their article outlines the specific behaviors that patrons found to be unhelpful and behaviors that patrons felt were helpful. These two researchers are building upon a rich research tradition that can trace its beginnings through the work of Durrance[2], Gers[3], Crowley[4] and Childers[5]. It is a tradition which has yielded some of the profession's most fruitful research. For example, the research conducted by the investigators identified six observable behaviors which increased reference accurarcy. This research was used as the basis for a statewide reference training program which resulted in reference accuracy in the state of Maryland increasing from 55 percent to 77 percent.[6]

Shearer and Bracy are continuing this rich research tradition in the area of readers' advisory service, as reported in this book. Their studies mirror the work of Durrance, Ross, and Dewdney. Like Gers, they are begining to identify those specific, observable behaviors that result in more effective readers' advisory service. Their finding that patrons express a higher satisfaction with readers' advisory transactions when the librarian elicits the patron's reaction to a recently read title is significant. Yet an important component of both the reference and readers advisory transaction is missing from all of these studies. While each of these studies provides illuminating information about the patron's experience and the librarian's observable behaviors, they do not provide much information about the librarian's experience of these transactions or about how librarian's think through providing readers' advisory service. This "how-to" knowledge is especially important in an area like readers' advisory service; it becomes critical when one realizes that resources in the area of readers' advisory work are few, that the transaction is frequently brief, and that the primary resource used is the librarian's personal knowledge of adult fiction.

In order to increase our understanding of the readers' advisory transaction, the author asked two other librarians to join him in analyzing a reader's interests, suggesting titles that might be of interest to this reader, explaining why these titles might be of interest to the reader, and identifying how they learned about these titles. These readers' advisors were also asked to examine each other's recommendations and to review the reader's reaction to all of the suggested titles.

The reader in this study is a white female who has earned several college degrees. She is currently employed as a health care professional in a medical center that is affiliated with a major university. She was asked to tell me about a book she had read and enjoyed. Her statement was videotaped and this investigator, along with two other librarians, reviewed her tape and suggested some titles she might like to read. These recommendations came to her in the form of a brief narrative description of each suggested title and a series of questions regarding her reaction to it. The reader viewed this exercise as something that would be "fun" and might result in her finding some new books to read. The author opened the taping session by using a question that is suggested by Joyce Saricks in her book *Readers' Advisory Service in the Public Library*.[7] That question is "Tell me about a book you've read and enjoyed." This is the reader's response to that question:

I think one of my favorite books of all time was a biography of Vita Sackville-West. I liked it because she was a very quirky lady who led a very quirky lifestyle and I like reading about people who have made unusual choices and had unusual lifestyles. I like very personal novels or personal books about real individuals or people who seem real and have grappled with tough choices. And when I think about other books I like—I think they all fall into that kind of category.

I read a book recently called *The Object of My Affection* and that's about a woman who lives with a male roomate and she gets pregnant by her former boyfriend and tries to decide whether to keep the child or not. And the male roomate happens to be gay and they have a very complicated relationship. And so the book is about their relationship and her decision to do something independently.

A nonfiction book that kinda fits into that category recently is Jill Conway's biography. The added dimension in that book is that it talks about a woman and her decision about pursuing an education in a time and place where that wasn't a fashionable thing to do. Again, it is a very personal novel—it is not action oriented but it talks a lot about personal change and nonconventional choices. So I think I'm pretty boring in that respect because over and over again those are the novels I like to read.

Advisor No. 1:

My Analysis:
This reader gives us three different selections—one biography, one novel, and one autobiography. All three are about women who have made nontraditional choices either in their personal lives or professional lives or both. The reader has indicated an interest in character and not in "action-oriented" writing. These are the factors that I am going to use in making my selections. I am going to look for novels that have women protagonists and that deal with relationships and nontraditional life choices. I am also going to focus my attention on mainstream fiction and not genre fiction. My reason-

ing here is that in mainstream fiction the focus of the work is usually an exploration of a character and the character's experiences. Even though the reader mentioned two "life stories," I am going to keep my initial recommendations to fiction.

My initial suggestions are:

Fannie Flagg's *Fried Green Tomatoes at the Whistle-Stop Cafe.* This title examines the relationship between two young women and the relationship between the older woman narrating their story and the woman at mid-life who hears it. I feel that this book might appeal to this reader because of its focus on several unusual women and the relationships that develop among them. I have read reviews of this book and seen the movie.

Elizabeth Hailey's *A Woman of Independent Means.* I have read this book and its main character is an interesting if not altogether positive heroine. Even though she lives a fairly traditional life—her articulation of it is anything but traditional. Also because the story is told entirely through letters written by the protagonist—the reader is constantly having to "read between the lines" to determine whether or not the heroine is a credible narrator. While this character may not be "quirky" enough for this reader, this book is a thoughtful examination of one woman's life.

Barbara Kingsolver's *The Bean Trees.* This is another title I have read. Kingsolver's heroine Taylor Greer is one of the most quirky, funny, and lovable women I have ever encountered in literature. Given the reader's interest in women and women who make nontraditional choices, I feel that this title should be of interest to the reader. Also this title elaborates on the "nontraditional" mother theme that the reader mentions as part of her description of *The Object of My Affection.*

Reynolds Price's *Kate Vaiden.* I have heard several individuals discuss the book and I have read reviews of it. It's heroine is another example of the strong woman who makes unusual choices. Again there is a link between this title and *The Object of My Affection* in that the main character develops a relationship with a gay male. My suggestion of this title to this reader is based on this link and the discussion of the main character as a woman who makes nontraditional choices.

Advisor No. 2:

Analysis:

She described books that are character driven: it seemed to me that character was the most important item to her. Her examples were mostly women, mostly nonfiction and biography. She said she liked nonconventional women and quirky characters. She also mentioned women who had struggled to overcome obstacles, in specifically higher education. (I did not use any readers' advisory tools as part of this exercise.)

Suggestions:

Nonfiction:

My first suggestion, which if she hasn't yet read it, is a good bet: *True North* by Jill Conway. This picks up Ms. Conway's story from the book the reader mentioned as her favorite. *The Road From Coorain.* (Biography.)

Next, I would suggest *The Power and the Passion of M. Carey Thomas* by Helen Horowitz—the biography of an amazing woman who became president of Bryn Mawr (strong, unusual, complicated woman character in higher education).

There is a new bio of Vannessa Redgrave, which if the fiction books below didn't work, I would hope this was in the library when the reader came back after reading the above!

I might also try and see if she would be interested in *Having Our Say* by the Delaney sisters. This is the story of two African American women, one now over 100, one deceased who are real characters in every sense of the word. Both were pioneers, one being the first African American and woman dentist in New York City.

Fiction:

When I think of quirky characters, I always first think of *The Accidental Tourist* by Anne Tyler. As the review says, even the dog is eccentric! Oldie but goodie.

A new book I haven't read but has good reviews is *Antarctic Navigation* by Elizabeth Arthur. Woman character of vision and drive.

A book that reminded me of *The Object of My Affection* is *Maybe the Moon* by Armistead Maupin. Again a straight woman and her gay friend, but this time the woman is only 31 inches tall. If she liked this, then I would recommend starting *The Tales of the City* series, which I personally liked way more than this. But I don't think she would try them with out liking something else Armistead wrote, because they are so unusual. (But they sure have quirky characters!)

I would also recommend *Smilla's Sense of Snow* by Peter Hoeg. Because it is unlike any other book I've read and I don't know anyone who didn't like it. A most unusual woman character, so I would suggest it . . . I know I'm imposing my taste on others . . .

Others that ran through my head as possibilities were:
Robber Bride by Margaret Atwood (strong, different women)
Bastard Out of Carolina by Dorothy Allison (which I have not read)
On the Stroll by Alex Kate Shulman (bag lady, gay boy, strange characters)

Advisor No. 3

Since the purpose of this exercise (as I understand it) is to provide an example of my readers' advisory process, I tried to strike a middle ground between a "library school" readers' advisory experience (i.e., "Your assignment is to recommend three titles for this patron. It's due in a couple of weeks. Use a variety of reference works and reviewing sources.") and a "real world"/direct service readers' advisory experience (i.e., "My kid's story hour will be oven in about ten minutes and I'd like to check out something for myself when I leave. What do you recommend?"). In library school, I might spend some time perusing the index of *Book Review Digest* and scanning some bibliographies and reviews. As I said, I tried to strike a middle ground.

I also found it strange not to have the patron there with me. In the "real world," this would be a two person process, a conversation. I would suggest some titles and, based upon the patron's reaction and comments, I would refine my process.

Having said that, here are my reactions to the patron's comments:

She described three books which she's enjoyed: a biography of Vita Sackville-West, a novel entitled *The Object of My Affection*, and *The Road from Coorain*, an autobiography by Jill Kerr Conway. Naturally, I immediately noted the fact that two of the three titles were biographical (even though, at one point, she referred to all three titles as "novels" she's enjoyed). After describing the first book, she said that she liked books about "real people" or "people who seem real."

There were two themes that recurred as the patron described these books. First, she described each as "personal"— even though she described the plot of the novel, she sounded as though she responded more to the characters than the plot. Second, she described each book in turn as being about "quirky," independent people who make "unusal"/tough"/ "nonconventional" choices. Although she didn't explicitly state it, I noted the fact that the two biographies were of women and, although the novel is about a woman living with a gay male roommate, the patron focused on the character of the woman—her situation and her decision.

What titles would I suggest? Well, my first thought was, "Uh, oh!" Because I don't read biographies, I couldn't make any personal recommendations. (My first step is usually to mentally review my readings for a title to recommend.) A few fiction titles, however, did immediately come to mind, either because I read them or because a friend read them and told me about them or because I remembered reading reviews of them.

All three of Sue Miller's novels: *The Good Mother, Family Pictures*, and *For Love* are primarily character studies with characters, usually women, facing difficult choices. *Family*

Pictures (the only one of the three which I've read) is a family story but, as I recall, the story is told/filtered through the eyes of one of the daughters. While my wife was reading the other two, she described them to me and they sound like something this patron might enjoy—after hearing of the plot of *Object of My Affection* I thought the complex situation in which *The Good Mother* finds herself might be especially interesting.

Having read both of Harriett Doerr's novels (i.e., *Stones for Ibarra* and *Consider This, Senora*), I would highly recommend both to the patron. While females are at the center of each, there are a number of fascinating and memorable characters (many of them women) to whom I think the patron would respond—strong, independent characters who "seem real."

I would also recommend a couple of other novels which I've read: Alice Hoffman's *At Risk* and Wallace Stegner's *Crossing to Safety*. While there are multiple characters at the cores of these two books (a family in the former and two married couples, one of which involves a "quirky" and "independent" woman, in the latter), I think the depth of the character studies would be appealing to the patron.

As far as biographies are concerned, while I haven't read them myself, I would mention to the patron a couple of biographies that I've heard/read about. Of course, I would want to be sure that she knew that Jill Kerr Conway had continued her autobiography in *True North*. I would say that I hadn't read it myself, but that, while I've seem some mixed reviews, many were positive. I would also describe *Having Our Say: The Delaney Sisters' First 100 Years* as an autobiography of two very strong and independent black women that, as I recall, was very well reviewed.

Now here's where it gets a little tricky. If I were really working with a patron, I would go with her to the biography section. On the way, I would be thinking of strong, independent women (e.g., Isak Dinesen, Georgia O'Keeffe). I would look for works on those women and I would scan the shelves and put some faith in serendipity. If I found any works with which I was absolutely unfamiliar, I would say that while I couldn't say anything about the quality, she might be interested in looking at them. As I said earlier, based upon her reactions/comments, I might revise my recommendations.

Since I didn't have the time pressure of working directly with a patron in the stacks in this case, I did something that's more a "library school" experience than a "real world" one (i.e., while I probably should, I probably wouldn't take the time while working with a patron to do this): I checked *The Readers' Adviser* for recommended biographies of some of the women (i.e., Dinesen and O'Keeffe) that came to mind.

I also did something I would do in the real world: I asked others. In the "real world," I would ask other librarians who might be working with me. For this exercise, I asked co-workers and friends for recommendations. I discovered that I don't know any biography readers! (I wonder: was this patron selected deliberately because her reading tastes would make this challenging?) However, when I described the parameters (i.e., biographies of "quirky" and/or "independent" women) a colleague said that a friend of hers enjoyed *Me* by Katharine Hepburn and *My Name Is Anna* by Patty Duke. I have some doubts that this particular patron would respond positively to these two titles so, while I might mention them, I wouldn't "recommend" them.

I also took a few minutes to leaf through some of the "best books" lists for 1994 (*Wilson Library Bulletin, Booklist, New York Times Book Review*). However, the only works I found were ones I'd already thought of.

Finally, as it does so often in the "real world," serendipity came to my rescue: while looking for a review of one of the above titles, I chanced across a "starred" review of Harriet Beecher Stowe. Perhaps the patron would find it interesting . . .

While I've named multiple titles for some of the authors above, I would recommend only one title for each author and say something like, "And if you enjoy this, there are others by this same author that you might enjoy."

Here is my final list:

Conway, Jill Kerr	*True North*
Delaney, Sarah and A. Elizabeth	*Having Our Say: The Delaney Sisters' First 100 Years*
Doerr, Harriet	*Consider This, Senora*
Hedrick, Joan D.	*Harriet Beecher Stowe: A Life*
Hoffman, Alice	*At Risk*
Miller, Sue	*Family Pictures*
Robinson, Roxana	*Georgia O'Keeffe: A Life*
Stegner, Wallace	*Crossing to Safety*
Thurman, Judith	*Isak Dinesen: The Life of a Storyteller*

After each advisor had provided me with a list of their suggestions and reviews for each of their suggested titles, this information was used to develop a reader reaction form for each title. These forms were given to the reader and she completed each form. All of these forms were then given to each advisor for their reaction and comments. (The reviews, from standard review media, and the reader's reactions to them may be read in the appendix to this chapter.)

Before going on to each advisor's reaction to these forms, a brief examination of one or two of these forms and the information they contain is in order. During any readers' advisory transaction, the advisor has an opportunity to extend the information gathering portion of the transaction. This opportunity occurs when the reader reacts to the advisor's intial suggestion or suggestions.

Of particular interest is the reader's reaction to Armisted Maupin's *Maybe the Moon* and Sue Miller's *Family Pictures*. The advisors who suggested these titles had good reasons for each suggestion. In the case of the Maupin title, this book contained "quirky" characters and a wide range of interpersonal relationships. In the case of Miller's work, the story concerns "real people in a real life" situation. In both cases, however, the reader's reaction to these titles gives the advisor much more information about what exactly the words "quirky" and "real" mean for this particular reader. For example, in *Maybe the*

Moon the reader states that "The characters don't appeal to me." While she doesn't elaborate on this, the consensus among the advisors in this investigation is that these characters are not "real" enough to meet this patron's requirements. An examination of the reader's reaction to other titles indicates a strong preference for stories about "real" people dealing with "real" life issues and choices. The reader's reaction to Sue Miller's book is also interesting. The reader says she might read *Family Pictures,* but she goes on to say that "the story of a "regular" family appeals to me less than the story of an "alternative family." The reader's reaction to this title reinforces her interest in "quirky" or "unusual" or "alternative" characters and situations. Taken together the reader's reaction to these two titles paints a picture of a reader who is interested in exploring characters who live in a realistically framed world but who are making nontraditional choices or dealing with nontraditional situations and lifestyles.

Each of the advisors in this study learned something from the reader's reaction to their suggested titles and the suggestions of their colleagues. As a result of their analysis of these reactions, each advisor "reframed" his or her view of the reader and used this information to begin to develop ideas for other titles and authors they might suggest to this reader. The reactions and comments of each advisor appear below. See the appendix at the end of this chapter for reader's reactions.

Advisor No. 1:

> I think the thing that was most interesting about this reader was the way her values emerge as I looked at her reactions. She certainly reinforces and elaborates on themes she mentioned in her description of books she has read and enjoyed. She is certainly interested in books which focus on women, which deal with unusual choices and lifestyles. Her interest in academic settings also emerges as she moves through these titles. This is one of the most striking elements to me of her reactions. She mentions it over and over in making her choices. It even plays a role in her deciding to read Wallace Stegner's *Crossing to Safety*.
>
> I also noticed that in my selections and the selections of

my colleagues that we all stayed away from "genre" titles. All of our selections were either mainstream fiction or biography. All of our titles were also well reviewed. This fits with the reader's focus on "character" and "personal stories."

As a result of examining these reactions, I would certainly add biographies to my next set of titles and preferably biographies about successful women. For example one title I might suggest is Mary Catherine Bateson's *Composing a Life*. This is an examination of the lives of several successful women and the life experiences they shared in becoming successful. Another reason for suggesting this title would be its discussion of Bateson's own life and that of Johnetta Cole (the first women president of Spelman College). Both of these "chapters" focus on how these women "composed" a life for themselves in academe.

Advisor No. 2:

In general there were not too many surprises. I felt that the reader's choices reinforced her statements about wanting stories about "real people" facing "real life" choices and issues. Her choices also emphasize her focus on women. It was interesting to me that in several cases (specifically Anne Tyler's *The Accidental Tourist* and Sue Miller's *Family Pictures*), when a novel had a male protagonist or focused on a "traditional" family, that the reader was not as interested in these titles. I also think that her interest in "real people" in "real life" is emphasized by her rejection of Maupin's *Maybe the Moon*. When she says that this novel's characters don't interest her, I think she may be saying that these characters are not realistic enough for her.

I found the reader's comments about *Consider This, Senora*, to be very interesting. Her statements about "life at a slower pace" and "detailing the small events in life" seem like new information to me. If we were engaged in an actual transaction, I might use this new information to make some different suggestions from the ones I made.

Another case where the reader's reaction would have been helpful to me was her response to *The Power and Passion of M. Carey Thomas.* She says "I'm interested in stories of the Seven Sisters and of successful women." I would have used this reaction to find more biographies about women who were involved in and influenced these schools. Her selection of the Harriet Beecher Stowe biography is also interesting. It is especially so, since her reaction to the other two biographies of women (Isak Dinesen and Georgia O'Keeffe) appear to be neutral. Based on her reaction to all four titles, I would definitely lean more toward biographies of women but stick to women in education, or who were involved in political or social movements. I also think that I would want biographies that focused on these women's successes and not their failures. I think a possible reason for this reader's reaction to the O'Keeffe biography may be its emphasis on the artist's last days as a "helpless" woman.

As I was looking through these responses, it also occurred to me that an author I should have suggested would have been May Sarton and her journals. I think these books might meet the reader's interests in "real women" making "real life" choices.

Advisor No. 3

I am pleased with this reader's reactions to the titles I suggested. In general, there were no surprises for me in this reader's reactions. Her reactions appear to be consistent with her statements about what she liked in the titles she mentioned. She likes books about women and alternative families and books that take place in an academic environment. In some ways her reactions really make her preferences clearer.

I was, however, especially interested in her reaction to the Sue Miller title. I suggested the Sue Miller title to see if she would be interested in it. I was aware of her earlier statements about women making "unusual choices" and books which discuss "unusual lifestyles." So I knew that I was taking a chance with the a book about a "traditional" family. I thought, however, that the unusual circumstances (i.e., dealing with a special child) might appeal to this reader. When she says that she is not interested in a "regular" family in her reaction to this title—that really got my attention. If this had been an actual tranasction, her reaction to this title would have sent me down a different path. I would have begun suggesting titles which focus more on "alternative" families and lifestyles.

Her reaction to Maupin's *Maybe the Moon* was also interesting because it deals with a lot of quirky characters and alternative lifestyles. I feel, however, that one of the reasons this title and its characters do not appeal to this reader is because of the overall tone of the book. She is really interested in stories that are "realistically" framed. Stories about real life and real people. The review for *Maybe the Moon* makes the characters appear like they are "soap opera" characters or are somehow larger (or "shorter") than real life. I feel that this may be one of the reasons this reader is not interested in this title

Other reactions I found interesting were the reader's reaction to the Anne Tyler title. What I learned from this reaction is that writing style does sometimes influence this reader and her reaction to a specific story or author. I was also struck by how many times this reader referred to nonprint media as a source of information about a title. For example, she has seen movie versions of the Anne Tyler and Fannie Flagg titles. She also noted that the Hailey title had recently been aired on TV.

After reviewing all of these titles and the reader's reaction to them, I would like the opportunity to sit down and discuss with my colleagues their choices and how they felt about this reader's reaction to their selections. I am particularly interested in the selection of *Smilla's Sense of Snow*. I really enjoyed that title but it is not one that I felt would fit for this reader based on the information I have about her.

Finally, I would like to say that while I enjoyed the "exercise" and found it useful and enlightening, I also found it very frustrating. For example, I didn't have the opportunity to modify my choices based on the reader's reactions while I was in the process of working with her. In that way, I think this process has an "artificial" feel to it. It's like doing readers' advisory work by e-mail instead of the way I would normally do it.

The Readers' Advisory Transaction

The readers' advisor basically has four tasks in any given transaction:

1. The advisor must elicit information about the reader's interests.
2. The advisor must have developed a style of thinking about books that looks for the similarities and links between titles and not just their uniqueness.
3. The advisor must be able to establish links between titles based on the reader's interests and the advisor's knowledge of titles and readers' advisory resources.
4. The advisor must be able to present identified titles and communicate how each title relates to the reader's interest.

Both Saricks[8] and Chelton[9] have provided a good grounding in questions to ask during the readers' advisory transaction. Sarick's "Tell me about a book you have read and enjoyed" elicits information that is easily accessible to the reader and yields a response that is extremely useful to the readers' advisor. It also asks the reader to provide information about their reading experience and, as noted by Shearer, readers rate transactions in which their opinions of their reading have been elicited higher than transactions where their opinons have not been elicited.

In terms of thinking about books, Saricks and Chelton again provide guidance for readers' advisory transaction. Both stress the need to pay attention to the genre in which the reader is reading as well as other elements such as character, the time in which the novel takes place, the geographic setting of the novel, and the novel's themes or subject. Another factor to consider is the novel's pacing. Saricks feels that pacing is one of the most important factors in locating titles of interest to a reader. Such factors as the "literariness" or "quality" of the writing, the balance between tragic elements of the story, and humor may also be significant factors for some readers. Whether or not a story contains sexually explicit scenes, violence, or "vulgar" language are also factors that sometimes come into play. These elements , however, cannot be viewed in isolation; they must be considered in the context of readers and their experiences. This is one of the reasons why eliciting the reader's experience of a particular title is a crucial part of the successful readers' advisory transaction.

As the advisors in this article have pointed out, the exercise in which they participated did not provide them with an opportunity to practice the first task of a readers' advisory transaction. That part was initially done for them. While each advisor was presented with an information rich transaction, advisor number three explicitly stated the "artificiality" of this exercise. What is interesting to note, however, is that while this advisor identifies his inability to gather more information from the reader, ask follow-up questions, and react to the reader's reaction to his suggestions in real time—this is the very sort of activity that is missing from most of the transactions identified as part of Bracy and Shearer's research. In their research, too many reader's advisory transactions have much more in common with a ready reference transaction than with the readers' advisory tranaction envisioned by advisor number three or the counselor role discussed by Kuhlthau in her book. The exercise in this article provides us with a new way of framing the readers' advisory transction. A "frame" that has more in common with Kuhlthau's imagined counselor role than the "ready reference" transaction that seems to be the most common one practice.

In her discussion of the counselor role, Kuhlthau provides the following description:

> The underlying assumption is that the user is learning from information in a constructive process as the information search process proceeds. There is no one right answer and no fixed sequence for all. The person's problem determines the intervention. The holistic experience is understood, acknowledged, and articulated as an important aspect of mediation. The user and the mediator enter into a dialogue.

The uncertainity principle underlies the Counselor's intervention. Information seeking is viewed as a process of construction rather than a quest for true answers. The user is guided through the dynamic and fluid process of seeking meaning. The recommended sequence of sources of information emerges as the topic or problem evolves in a highly individual way. The information is understood from the frame of reference of the users [sic] past experience and the constructs they hold. There are many meanings and many focuses within a general topic. The user forms a focus that is a personal perspective of the general topic under investigation. The Counselor approaches information seeking as a creative, individual process that is dynamic and unique for each person.[10]

While Kuhlthau is focusing on an "information" transaction, shifting a few words in her paragraphs allows us to overlay her statements onto the readers' advisory transaction. For example, in this exercise all advisors used the reader's past experience with books as the basis for making their suggestions. All three advisors used the reader's transcript to identify her interest in titles that were realistically framed, personal stories about women would made unusual decisions and choices, and sometimes were "quirky" characters engaged in unusual or alternative life choices. They then used this information to provide the reader with titles that had some or all of these elements. The advisors then used the reader's reaction to "test" and "refine" their hypotheses about what type or types of books that really interested the reader. Even in this "exercise" the advisors were engaged in an "dialogue" with the user using information she provided in her reactions to their suggestions to guide them to other titles. In this exercise, as in Kuhlthau's description of the counselor role, both the reader and the advisors came to a fuller understanding of the reader's unique view of what makes a book a good book.

Kuhlthau has indicated that much reflection and discussion of their practice is need to develop and elaborate the actual skills and tasks of the counselor. The same is true for the readers' advisor. Much more work is needed to fully elaborate the "model" of the readers' advisory transaction that is implied by this exercise. As the work progresses, we can only develop a fuller understanding of our readers, the texts in our collections and an understanding of the meaing of what we and our readers are seeking when they attempt to find their next book.

Notes

1. Ross, Catherine Sheldrick and Patricia Dewdney, "Best Practices: An Analysis of the Best (and Worst) in Fifty-Two Public Library Reference Transactions." *Public Libraries* vol. 33 (September/October 1994): 261–266.

2. Durrance, Joan C. "Reference Success: Does the 55% Rule Tell the Whole Story?" *Library Journal* 114 (April 15, 1989): 31–36.

3. Gers, Ralph and Lillie Seward, "Improving Reference Performance: Results of a Statewide Study," *Library Journal* vol. 110 (November 15, 1985): 32–35.

4. Crowley, Terrence "Half-Right Reference: Is it True?" *RQ* vol 25 (Fall 1985): 59–68.

5. Childers, Thomas "Telephone Information Service in Public Libraries: A Comparison of Performance and the Descriptive Statistics Collected by the State of New Jersey" (PhD dissertation, Rutgers University, 1970).

6. Stephan, Sandy et. al., "Reference Breakthrough in Maryland," *Public Libraries* vol. 27 (Winter, 1988): 202–203.

7. Saricks, Joyce and Nancy Brown, *Readers' Advisory Services in the Public Library* (Chicago, IL: American Library Association, 1989): 33.

8. Ibid.

9. Chelton, Mary K. "Read Any Good Books Lately? Helping Patrons Find What They Want," *Library Journal* vol. 116 (May 1, 1993): 33–37.

10. Kuhlthau, Carol Collier. *Seeking Meaning: A Process Approach to Library and Information Services* (Norwood, NJ: Ablex Publishing Corporation, 1993): 143.

Appendix

This appendix contains the reader's reaction sheets referred to in the article. The summaries of the novels are the summaries that the reader responded to. In addition to these summaries several questions relating to the reader's experience with a particular author and title are also provided; reader's responses are in italics.

Author: Arthur, Elizabeth

Title: *Antartcic Navigation*

Genre: General Fiction

Summary: In a triumph of the novelist's art, Arthur (*Looking for the Klondike Stone*) brings a wide-ranging intelligence and curiosity, a compelling skill in character portrayal and a moral gravity to this 800-page story of human quest. In chronicling the growing obsession of her heroine, Morgan Lamont, to recreate the doomed 1910 Antartctic Expedition of Robert Falcon Scott, Arthur painstakingly develops Morgan's complex character, credibly establishing her spiritual kinship with the failed explorer and her determination to understand the true meaning of his journey. (Source: *Publishers Weekly,* November 21, 1994, page 69, reprinted with permission.)

Have you heard of this author? *No.*
Have you read any books by this author? *No.*
Have you heard of this title? *No.*
Have you read this title? *No.*
Which of the following best describes your reaction to this title?
____ I would definitely read/borrow this book at some time.
____ I might read/borrow this book at some time.
____ I probably would not read/borrow this book at any time.
 _X_ I defintiely would not read/borrow this book at any time.
Do you need more information about this title? *No.*
What about this book appeals or does not appeal to you? *Story of an expedition not immediately appealing.*

Author:	Conway, Jill Ker
Title:	*True North: A Memoir*
Genre:	Biography
Summary:	In this memoir Conway picks up where she left off in *Road From Coorain* (1989). She recounts her life in America from her arrival in 1960 up to her appointment to the presidency of Smith College in 1975. Conway comes to the United States to pursue her interest in history and escape Australian society, which has no place for a woman academic. She conveys her first impressions and wonderment at the American way of life, from its ethnic diversity to its stale packaged bread to what Conway considers to be the disarming emotional frankness of Americans. Pursuing her studies at Harvard, she discovers a supportive intellectual community she had never before know. Studying American women reformers, she learns to identify passionately with those who defied social convention to bring women out of the confines of domesticity and into public life. Later, during her tenure at the University of Toronto, Conway experiences the difficulties of coping with her husband's manic-depression and her own inability to have children. At the same time, as the first woman in the university's senior administration, she finds she has become a public figure, a role model for feminists, and is frequently asked to speak at women's groups. Just as necessary funds are being cut at the university, Conway is asked to serve as president of Smith. She is most happy about the appointment because she finally will be able to properly champion women's education, which always has been one of the deepest concerns in her personal life and historical studies. Conway's life has been a fascinating, adventurous one. Yet the reader's sympathy may be tested by her frequent resort to benign ethnic stereotypes ("Gallic

joie de vivre," "the wildly extravagant humor" of Jews, "the Irishman's way with a story") as a substitute for the harder work of portraying individual characters. (Source: *Kirkus Reviews*, June 1, 1994, pages 749, reprinted with permission.)

Have you heard of this author? *Yes.*

Have you read any books by this author? *Yes.*

If YES, please describe your reaction to this author: *I loved her descriptions of the life and landscape of her youth in "The Road from Loorain."*

Have you heard of this title? *Yes.*

Have you read this title? *Yes.*

If YES, please describe your reaction to this title: *Her description of an academic woman was wonderful—I'd like to read more of this.*

Which of the following best describes your reaction to the title? *Not applicable since the reader has already read it.*

AUTHOR:	Delaney, Sarah, and A. Elizabeth
TITLE:	*Having Our Say: The Delaney Sisters' First 100 Years*
GENRE:	Biography
Citation:	*Wilson Library Bulletin*, December, 1994, page 28

Have you heard of this author? *Yes.*

Have you read any books by this author? *No.*

Have you heard of this title? *Yes.*

If YES, please describe what you have heard: *Read a review in the local paper.*

Have you read this title? *No.*

Which of the following best describes your reaction to this title?

____ I would definitely read/borrow this book at some time.

 X I might read/borrow this book at some time.

____ I probably would not read/borrow this book at any time.

____ I definitely would not read/borrow this book at any time.

Do you need more information about this title? *No.*

What about this book appeals or does not appeal to you? *The story of a relationship between women, and story of women who never married, appeals to me.*

AUTHOR: Doerr, Harriet

TITLE: *Consider This, Senora*

GENRE: General Fiction

Summary: It's been 10 years since Doerr dazzled us with the *Stones of Ibarra*, a suitably long and reflective interlude considering that waiting is the theme of her lovely second novel. As Ursula Bowles, the senior member of a small group of Americans living in Mexico, observes, the Spanish word for waiting and hoping are one and the same, a truth Doerr explicates with subtlety and adroitness. Ursula, nearly 80 when the story begins, has returned to Mexico, the land of her childhood, to await her death. She and her daughter, Fran meet Susanna Ames, a young, exquisite, and freshly divorced artist determined to let the gorgeous sky and untrampeled land of Mexico aborb her battered soul. To this end, she enters into a risky property deal with another American, a complete stranger on the lam from the IRS and eager to make a quick buck. Together, they buy the run-down family estate of Don Enrique Ortiz. Grace personified, Sue beautifies everything she comes in contact with, from failing gardens to starving children. Doerr, in prose as meticulous as knitting and warm and brilliant as sunlight, traces the interactions of the unusual Americans with the people of the village and creates a chain of incidents that, ultimately, celebrates every facet of life, from desire and love to despair and death. Doerr instills each of her memorable characters with great dignity and resilience, and bestows upon her entranced readers a deep sense of peace and wonder. (Source: *Booklist*, June 1 & 15, 1993, page 1734, reprinted with permission.)

Have you heard of this author? *Yes.*

Have you read any books by this author? *No.*

Have you heard of this title? *No.*

Have you read this title? *No.*
Which of the following best describes your reaction to this title?
__X__ I would definitely read/borrow this book at some time.
_____ I might read/borrow this book at some time.
_____ I probably would not read/borrow this book at any time.
_____ I definitely would not read/borrow this book at any time.
Do you need more information about this title? *No.*
What about this book appeals or does not appeal to you? *The story of life at a slower pace, detailing the small events in life that make up happiness and meaning appeals to me.*

AUTHOR:	Flagg, Fannie
TITLE:	*Fried Green Tomatoes at the Whistle-Stop Cafe*
GENRE:	General Fiction
Summary:	This novel is "set in a rural hamlet outside of Birmingham, Alabama." Bulletins from a gossipy town newsletter produced in the 1940s by Dot Weems are interspersed with the recollections of Mrs. Cleo (Vinnie) Throughgoode uttered (40 years later) in a nursing home to a depressed, menopausal visitor, Evelyn Couch (whose life is rejuvenated by these Sunday afternoon chats). Flagg also supplies basic narrative passages illuminating the news shared by Dot and Vinnie. The pace of the novel is as swift as the life of the small town is slow—at least it seems slow until Vinnie drops hints of a murder and of riotous pranks played upon the local minister. The story is carefully plotted, with the moods and people of pre- and post-World War II Alabama splendidly evoked. (Source: *Fiction Catalog*, 12th edition, page 210, H.W. Wilson, 1991, reprinted with permission.)

Have you heard of this author? *Yes.*
Have you read any books by this author? *No.*
Have you heard of this title? *Yes.*
If YES, please describe what you have heard about this title:
I saw the movie.

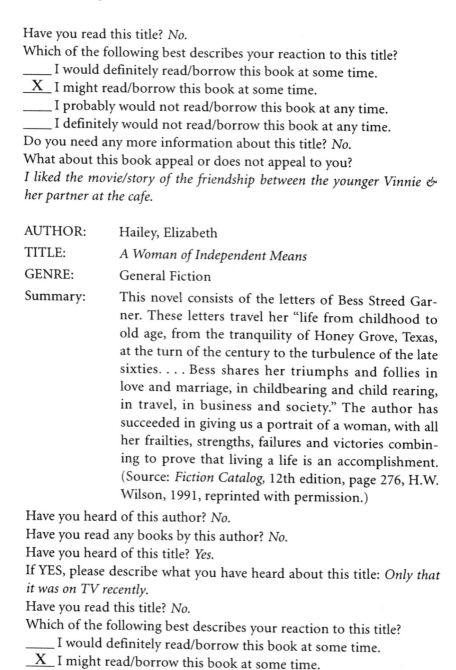

Have you read this title? *No.*

Which of the following best describes your reaction to this title?

____ I would definitely read/borrow this book at some time.

_X_ I might read/borrow this book at some time.

____ I probably would not read/borrow this book at any time.

____ I definitely would not read/borrow this book at any time.

Do you need any more information about this title? *No.*

What about this book appeal or does not appeal to you?

I liked the movie/story of the friendship between the younger Vinnie & her partner at the cafe.

AUTHOR: Hailey, Elizabeth

TITLE: *A Woman of Independent Means*

GENRE: General Fiction

Summary: This novel consists of the letters of Bess Streed Garner. These letters travel her "life from childhood to old age, from the tranquility of Honey Grove, Texas, at the turn of the century to the turbulence of the late sixties. . . . Bess shares her triumphs and follies in love and marriage, in childbearing and child rearing, in travel, in business and society." The author has succeeded in giving us a portrait of a woman, with all her frailties, strengths, failures and victories combining to prove that living a life is an accomplishment. (Source: *Fiction Catalog,* 12th edition, page 276, H.W. Wilson, 1991, reprinted with permission.)

Have you heard of this author? *No.*

Have you read any books by this author? *No.*

Have you heard of this title? *Yes.*

If YES, please describe what you have heard about this title: *Only that it was on TV recently.*

Have you read this title? *No.*

Which of the following best describes your reaction to this title?

____ I would definitely read/borrow this book at some time.

_X_ I might read/borrow this book at some time.

____ I probably would not read/borrow this book at any time.

____ I definitely would not read/borrow this book at any time.

Do you need more information about this title? *No.*

What about this book appeals or does not appeal to you? *I like the idea of a story of a woman's life, told from the main character's perspective.*

AUTHOR:	Hedrick, Joan D.
TITLE:	*Harriet Beecher Stowe: A Life*
GENRE:	Biography
Summary:	It's been 50 years since the last biography of the once adulated, eventually maligned author of *Uncle Tom's Cabin* (1852), Harriet Beecher Stowe, was published and it's high time for a new look at this hugely influential writer. Hedrick, a dynamic social and literary historian, has made great use of previously unavailable materials and written a far-reaching and brilliantly synthesized narrative that not only relates Stowe's complex personal story, but also captures the ferment and verve of America's antebellum era. Born in 1811 into the industrious evangelical Beecher family of Massachusetts, Stowe came of age in unison with the emergence of America's fledgling national consciousness. After receiving an unusually thorough education for a woman of her time, Stowe began her writing life in the thriving frontier city of Cincinnati, winning over magazine readers with her conversational tone, acute observations, pioneering use of dialect, shrewd irony, and unabashed melodrama. As Hedrick tracks Stowe's progress from a scribbler of "parlor literature" to a world-renowned novelist and abolitionist, she makes certain that we understand just how much the status of women and the lack of reliable birth control shaped Stowe's daily life and moral outlook. It was the trauma of the deaths of several of her seven children that sensitized Stowe to the horrors of slave life and inspired her most famous

work. A major achievement, this respectful and empathic portrait illuminates a crucial figure in our history. (Source: *Booklist*, January 15, 1994, page 893, reprinted with permission.)

Have your heard of this author? *Yes.*

Have you read any books by this author? *No.*

Have you heard of this title? *No.*

Have you read this title? *No.*

Which of the following best describe your reaction to this title?

__X__ I would definitely read/borrow this book at some time.

_____ I might read/borrow this book at some time.

_____ I probably would not read/borrow this book at any time.

_____ I definitely would not read/borrow this book at any time.

Do you need more information about this title? *No.*

What about this book appeals or does not appeal to you? *Biography of a woman.*

AUTHOR:	Hoeg, Peter
TITLE:	*Smilla's Sense of Snow*
GENRE:	General Fiction
Summary:	Danish novelist Hoeg's first English-language publication is an attempt to freeze out *Gorky Park* by moving from an intimate mystery to an ever-widening circle of corruption and danger—and to even colder climes. Surly Inuit/Greenlander Smilla Jaspersen is a world-class expert on ice and snow who, since emigrating to Denmark, has gone on nine scientific expeditions to her homeland and published half a dozen highly regarded papers in scholarly journals—but she still can't hold a steady job. When Isaiah Christensen, her six-year-old downstairs neighbor with a long-standing fear of heights, plunges from the roof of the White Palace, their apartment building, Smilla presses for a police inquiry; but instead of a homicide detective, the police send an investigator from the fraud division. Why? Also, why did somebody per-

form a muscle biopsy on Isaiah after he died? What was he doing on that roof in the first place? And what does his death have to do with his father's death on an expedition to Greenland two years before—a death that, Smilla learns from extravagantly pious accountant Elsa Lbring, was recompensed by a full, unearned pension by the Cryolite Corporation? With the help of another neighbor, dyslexic mechanic Peter Fjl, Smilla follows a trail from the White Palace through the Cryolite records of a fateful (and fatal) 1966 expedition, and ends up aboard the *Kronos*, a smuggling ship stuffed with drugs and desperate characters and bound for Greenland's Barren Glacier and a truly unimaginable cargo. (Source: *Kirkus Reviews*, July 1, 1993, page 806, reprinted with permission.)

Have you heard of this author? *No.*
Have you read any books by this author? *No.*
Have you heard of this title? *No.*
Which of the following best describes your reaction to this title?
____ I would definitely read/borrow this book at some time.
X I might read/borrow this book at some time.
____ I probably would not read/borrow this book at any time.
____ I would definitely not read/borrow this book at any time.
Do you need more information about this title? *No.*
What about this book appeals or does not appeal to you? *I like the title, I like the idea of a mystery.*

AUTHOR:	Hoffman, Alice
TITLE:	*At Risk*
GENRE:	General Fiction
Summary:	When 11-year-old Amanda suffers from a particularly violent summer cold, the family doctor is summoned. This talented sixth-grade gymnast, who harbors dreams of the Olympics, is diagnosed with AIDS. When Amanda's father learns of his daughter's plight,

realizing that its cause is a blood transfusion necessitated by an emergency appendectomy five years earlier, he can hardly contain his fury at the doctor, the anonymous donor, and the random cruelty of the virus itself. With equal realism and intensity Hoffman exposes the similarly complex reactions of Amanda's mother, brother and grandparents, as well as the close New England community in which they live. Controversy rages over whether Amanda should be removed from school—with petitioners hawking their cause on the steps of the school building. Several parents—including the mother of Amanda's brother's best friend—remove their children from school. Meanwhile, an able princicpal attempts to assuage the fears of the public, protect her students (including Amanda), and answer the rebukes of her own children. Although Hoffman dramatizes a highly emotional, controversial issue, her novel is remarkably restrained and gracefully written. (Source: *Booklist*, May 15, 1988, page 1553, reprinted with permission.)

Have you heard of this author? *No.*
Have you read any books by this author? *No.*
Have you heard of this title? *No.*
Which of the following best describes your reaction to this title?
____ I would definitely read/borrow this book at some time.
_**X**_ I might read/borrow this book at some time.
____ I probably would not read/borrow this book at any time.
____ I definitely would not read/borrow this book at any time.
Do you need more information about this title? *No.*
What about this book appeals or does not appeal to you? *Sounds like a powerful forum to explore a complicated, current issue.*

AUTHOR: Horowitz, Hele Lefkowitz
TITLE: *The Power and Passion of M. Carey Thomas*
GENRE: Biography
Summary: A lengthy biography of educator M. Carey Thomas

(1857–1935). Horowitz (*History & American Studies/ Smith: Campus Life*, 1987, etc.) presents Thomas as a "bundle of conflicting aspirations," a woman torn betweeen scholarship, women's education and art. Born in Baltimore in 1857 to Quaker parents, Thomas showed, early in life, an ambition to break through the social constraints placed on women. She studies abroad, was the first women to earn summa cum laude honors for her Ph.D. from the University of Zurich, and then set her sights on the presidency of newly founded Bryn Mawr College for Women. After settling for the position of dean of Bryn Mawr at the age of 27, Thomas concentrated on education, sadly putting aside her own research and art, a compromise that continued after her ascendency to the presidency ten years later. Although Horowitz practically apologizes for Thomas's turn to political conservatism and bureaucratic manipulations later in life, the educator shone as she struggled to succeed in a world not usually friendly to women. Horowitz follows her passionate affairs with women, primarily with long-time friend Mamie Gwinn and heiress Mary Garrett. When her 25-year relationship with Gwinn ended, Thomas experienced desperate pain, even though the affluent Garrett was waiting in the wings. Thomas's anti-Semitism and racism, certainly not a pretty part of the picture, are eclipsed in this account by her intense ambition and obsession with monetary gain. At 65, quite wealthy since Garrett willed the bulk of her estate to her, and after serving 28 years as president of Bryn Mawr, Thomas retired once again to pursue her love of art and travel. At times burdened by its unrelenting attention to detail, Horowitz's account personalizes a courageous woman and provides the historical context to balance her complex and contradictory life choices. (Source: *Kirkus Reviews*, June 15, 1994, page 822, reprinted with permission.)

Have you heard of this author? *No.*
Have you read any books by this author? *No.*
Have you heard of this title? *No.*
Have you read this title? *No.*
Which of the following best describes your reaction to this title?
__X__ I would definitely read/borrow this book at some time.
_____ I might read/borrow this book at some time.
_____ I probably would not read/borrow this book at any time.
_____ I definitely would not read/borrow this book at any time.
Do you need more information about this title? *No.*
What about this book appeals or does not appeal to you? *I'm interested in stories of the Seven Sisters & of successful ambitious women.*

AUTHOR:	Kingsolver, Barbara
TITLE:	*The Bean Trees*
GENRE:	General Fiction
Summary:	In this novel, "Taylor Greer, a poor, young woman, flees her Kentucky home and heads west . . . While passing through Oklahoma, she becomes responsible for a two-year-old Cherokee girl. The two continue on the road. When they roll off the highway in Tucson, Taylor and the child, whom she has named Turtle, . . . meet Mattie, a widow who runs Jesus Is Lord Used Tires and is active in the sanctuary movement on the side." Barbara Kingsolver can write. On any page of this accomplished first novel, you can find a striking image of fine dialogue or a telling bit of drama. (Source: *Fiction Catalog,* 12th edition, page 359, HW Wilson, 1991, reprinted with permission.)

Have you heard of this author? *Yes.*
Have you read any books by this author? *Yes.*
If YES, please describe your reaction to this author: *Positive—I like her flair for describing quirky situations and how characters find comfort in unusual relationships.*
Have you heard of this title? *Yes.*
If YES, please describe what you have heard about this title: *See next response.*

Have you read this title? *Yes.*
Which of the following best describes your reaction to this title? *Not applicable since I have already read the book!*
Do you need more information about this title? *No.*
What about this book appeals or does not appeal to you? *I enjoyed the story of an unusual family & of a person working through her demons.*

AUTHOR:	Maupin, Armistead
TITLE:	*Maybe the Moon*
GENRE:	General Fiction
Summary:	Maupin follows his fabulously funny, politically hip *Tale of the City* (the first successful serially published novel—indeed, series of novels—since God knows when) with the story of Cady Roth, the world's shortest female would-be movie star, who one inhabited the rubber corpus of the elf-protagonist of the second most popular movie in history, Mr. Woods, and who's been trying ever since to be recognized clad in her own skin and one of the outfits she's small enough to make out of a single yard of material. Her friends include a gay novelist-activist Jeff, her housemate Renee, who's the incarnation of the dumb blonde bombshell with a heart of gold, and Neil Riccarton, a young black divorced father struggling to make his way in showbiz, too. Eventually Cady and Neil get a thing going, as does Jeff with Cady's Mr. Woods costar Callum, now grown up into something of a gay preppy wet dream. By book's end, both romances have foundered, both on the rocks of fearful prejudice. And then, Cady gets a chance to avenge the wrongs Hollywood, particularly Mr. Woods' director Philip Blenheim (a Spielberg-Coppola type), has done her. Animated more by keen appreciation of the different yet similar injustices little people and gays suffer than by Maupin's daffy and endearing humor, *Maybe the Moon* is as easy to keep reading as any of

the *Tales*, but it's not as much fun. It is, however, arguably more affecting—a serious soap opera travesty that's exactly attuned to these times of increasing pressure for social equality. (Source: *Booklist*, September 15, 1992, Upfront Reviews, page 100, reprinted with permission.)

Have you heard of this author? *Yes.*

Have you read any books by this author? *Yes.*

If YES, please describe your reaction to this author: *Captured a time in SF well.*

Have you heard of this title? *No.*

Have you read this title? *No.*

Which of the following best describes your reaction to this title?

____ I would definitely read/borrow this book at some time.

____ I might read/borrow this book at some time.

_X_ I probably would not read/borrow this book at any time.

____ I definitely would not read/borrow this book at any time.

Do you need more information about this title? *No.*

What about this book appeals or does not appeal to you? *The characters don't appeal to me.*

AUTHOR:	Miller, Sue
TITLE:	*Family Pictures*
GENRE:	General Fiction
Summary:	If the expression multigenerational saga implies a work of fiction lacking in depth, then the latest novel by the author of the widely regarded *Good Mother* (*Booklist* Mr 1 86) will disabuse the reader of such a notion. Miller extends her tale over a 40-year period, following the full effect a special son has on the lives of not only his parents but also his siblings. David Eberhardt is a psychiatrist living with wife, Lainey, in the Hyde Park section of Chicago; their third child is autistic, and in rapid succession David and Lainey have three more children as a sort of compensation for little Randall's impairments. In a steady buildup

of sonorous detail—with good narrative tension without an ounce of sentimentality—Miller explores the ramifications of such an adjustment in all of those (mother, father, sisters, and brother) having to deal with the boy until the day he dies. (Source: *Booklist,* February 15, 1990, page 1121, reprinted with permission.)

Have you heard of this author? *Yes.*
Have you read any books by this author? *Yes.*
If YES, what was your reaction to this author? *Too long ago to remember.*
Have you heard of this title? *No.*
Have you read this title? *No.*
Which of the following best describes your reaction to this title?
____ I would definitely read/borrow this book at some time.
_X_ I might read/borrow this book at some time.
____ I probably would not read/borrow this book at any time.
____ I definitely would not read/borrow this book at any time.
Do you need more information about this title? *No.*
What about this book appeals or does not appeal to you? *Honestly— the story of a "regular" family appeals to me less than the story of an "alternative family."*

AUTHOR: Price, Reynolds
TITLE: *Kate Vaiden*
GENRE: General Fiction
Summary: In this novel, Kate Vaiden tells her own story "to justify herself to a son she abandoned as a baby and hasn't seen in 40 years." The decisive event in Kate's life occurred in 1938, when she was 11. Her father inexplicably murdered her mother and killed himself, leaving a letter that Kate doesn't read until many years later. . . . Kate is lovingly raised by a taciturn aunt and uncle with a secret sorrow she gradually learns: their homosexual son, Walter, ran off 12 years earlier with another local boy. When Walter comes

home on a visit, he befriends Kate, who later runs off to live with him and has a child by his lover. Mr. Price's successful creation of a female voice may be a tour de force, but it never feels like a showy ventriloquial act. Instead, Kate is a wholly convincing girl and a not improbable woman. (Source: *Fiction Catalog,* 12th edition, page 508, H.W. Wilson, 1991, reprinted with permission.)

Have you heard of this author? *Yes.*

Have you read any books by this author? *Yes.*

If YES, please desribe your reaction to this author: *Many deeply troubled characters.*

Have you heard of this title? *Yes.*

Have you read this title? *Yes.*

If YES, please describe your reaction to this title: *Loved it.*

Which of the following best describes your reaction to this title? *Not applicable since I've read it.*

Do you need more information about this title? *No.*

What about this book appeals or does not appeal to you? *I like the description of a woman's life, looking back, coming to terms & decisions.*

AUTHOR: Robinson, Roxana

TITLE: *Georgia O'Keeffe: A Life*

GENRE: Biography

Citation: *Time,* November 20, 1989, page 104

Have you heard of this author? *No.*

Have you read any books by this author? *No.*

Have you heard of this title? *No.*

Have you read this title? *No.*

Which of the following best describes your reaction to this title?

____ I would definitely read/borrow this book at some time.

__X_ I might read/borrow this book at some time.

____ I probably would not read/borrow this book at any time.

____ I definitely would not read/borrow this book at any time.

Do you need more information about this title? *No.*

What about this book appeals or does not appeal to you? *Biography of a successful woman appeals to me.*

AUTHOR: Stegner, Wallace

TITLE: *Crossing to Safety*

GENRE: General Fiction

Summary: This American writer celebrates a respected 50-year career with his latest novel, which is an appropriately autumnal consideration of life and human relationships. Two young couples from different backgrounds and regions meet in the academic backwater of a Wisconsin university. At first, they are excited by the future success they fantasize about, but soon they are confronted by the threat of scholastic failure and physcial illness. The bonds—both within the individual marriages and between the two couples—remain strong, and despite separation and disappointment, their friendships prosper until the prospect of death finally forces a brutal reconsideration of what life has handed these four people. Stegner writes from the heart as he poignantly shares his character's joys and sorrows, laughter and tears. (Source: *Booklist*, September 1, 1987, page 2, reprinted with permission.)

Have you heard of this author? *Yes.*

Have you read any books by this author? *Yes.*

If YES, please describe your reaction to this author: *Insightful.*

Have you heard of this title? *No.*

Have read this title? *No.*

Which of the following best describes your reaction to this title?

  X I would definitely read/borrow this book at some time.

____ I might read/borrow this book at some time.

____ I probably would not read/borrow this book at some time.

____ I definitely would not read/borrow this book at some time.

Do you need more information about this title? *No.*

What about this book appeals or does not appeal to you? *I like the idea of a story of relationships and like the setting—academic.*

AUTHOR: Thurman, Judith

TITLE: *Isak Dinesen: The life of a storyteller*

GENRE: Biography

Citation: *Library Journal,* October 15, 1982, page 1990

Have you heard of this author? *No.*

Have you read any books by this author? *No.*

Have you heard of this title? *No.*

Have you read this title? *No.*

Which of the following best describes your reaction to this title?

_____ I would definitely read/borrow this book at some time.

_X_ I might read/borrow this book at some time.

_____ I probably would not read/borrow this book at some time.

_____ I definitely would not read/borrow this book at some time.

Do you need more information about this title? *No.*

What about this book appeals or does not appeal to you? *Biography of prominent woman appeals.*

AUTHOR: Tyler, Anne

TITLE: *The Accidental Tourist*

GENRE: General Fiction

Citation: *Library Journal,* September 15, 1982, page 96

Have you heard of this author? *Yes.*

Have you read any books by this author? *Yes.*

If YES, please describe your reaction to this author: *Difficult to get through.*

Have you heard of this title? *Yes.*

If YES, please describe what you have heard: *Saw the movie.*

Have you read this title? *No.*

Which of the following best describes your reaction to this title?

_____ I would definitely read/borrow this book at some time.

_____ I probably would read/borrow this book at some time.

_X_ I probably would not read/borrow this book at some time.

_____ I definitely would not read/borrow this book at some time.

Do you need more information about this title? *No.*

What about this book appeals or does not appeal to you?

Idea appeals, writing somehow doesn't.

Part II:
The Environment of Readers' Advisory Service: Categorizing and Arranging Fiction Collections

Chapter Six:
A Decade's Worth of Research on Browsing Fiction Collections

by Sharon L. Baker

𝓕unding rates for today's public libraries seem especially low today, at a time when increases in the costs of library materials are outpacing those of inflation and when libraries must build comprehensive collections of materials like compact discs and videotapes that did not even exist twenty years ago, as well as invest in a wide variety of new technological equipment.

If we do not want the public library of the future to be a place where a story hour featuring *The Grinch Who Stole Christmas* becomes a luxury rather than a basic service, where a full-length book-on-tape of *A Tale of Two Cities* is replaced by an abridged version that omits its evocative opening line, and where patrons of all income levels must pay to "rent" any kind of material they want to borrow, it is imperative for us to undertake two tasks:

1. expand in the long-term both the base and depth of our fund-raising efforts; and
2. manage our existing resources as effectively as is possible.

A discussion of the first is beyond the scope of this paper. However, librarians can improve existing fiction collections, collections that, while logically organized for quick retrieval of *specific* titles, do not always enable browsing patrons to select, easily and successfully, works that they will like.

We can begin by searching out the research-based facts that illustrate the real success and failure rates of browsers.[1] These rates are often hidden, like low-growing succulent plants, in a rocky field.[2] The facts that do exist confirm our knowledge that a significant number of public library patrons choose their materials through browsing. For example, 49 percent of the patrons in a suburban Sydney public library had come to the library primarily to browse.[3] The proportion of browsers among fiction borrowers is even higher. For example, one study found that 86 percent of those who borrowed fiction had *not* used the catalog to help them with their selection.[4] And between 14 percent and 29 percent of borrowers select books for others—partners, children, and friends—as well as themselves.[5]

But facts relating to browsing success rates need to be considered in their larger context. One finding—that four out of five of the users surveyed in two British public libraries were satisfied to accept shelf arrangements as they were[6]—suggests that our regular patrons learn to use the organization systems we have provided them, just as shoppers learn the locations of items in their favorite grocery stores. However, it does not necessarily mean that further improvements of our existing shelf arrangements are unwarranted.

Other "facts" could mislead us unless we recognize the limitations of the survey instruments that generated them. For example, the Library Survey (materials availability form) from *Output Measures for Public Libraries* asks browsers whether they found *something* they were interested in. The lack of precision of this definition and the patron's inability to check a response like "partially," help explain why many of the libraries using this form report filling more than 90 percent of their patrons' browsing needs.[7] A more in-depth study, conducted in three British public libraries, also showed that 92 percent of those looking for fiction had borrowed something. But its authors suggested that librarians should not feel too complacent about this since 52 percent of these patrons had looked for certain authors *unsuccessfully*.[8]

In other words, there is a lot of substitution going on. Some of this substitution is good, since it introduces readers to new authors—

authors that they *are* often willing to try—at least once. But not all readers like the authors they choose in this fashion. One set of researchers found, for example, that readers who came browsing for specific authors already known by them were most likely to like the books they borrowed. In contrast, readers using the most common method of selection (browsing for "something" that looks interesting) were least likely to have enjoyed the books they had returned. In all, 18 percent of browsers did not enjoy the titles they read (most of these did not even finish the books). Another 22 percent were lukewarm, while 60 percent enjoyed the works they chose.[9]

Those who had not fully enjoyed a work expressed disappointment with the match between the work's content and style and their own reading tastes, often noting that that the work was not what they expected. This was often a result of lack of information about the work or an inaccurate assessment of its contents, series, or type in the brief time available to them for selection.

Success rates also need to be interpreted in light of studies that show that frustration is one of the primary emotions experienced by those who visit libraries.[10] Some browser frustration is related to the previously mentioned fact that browsers all too often say that the books they want are not on the shelves, that there are fewer current materials than they would like, and that they have run out of authors that they like.[11] But another significant part of their frustration reflects the fact that browsers find the *act* of browsing difficult in and of itself, since they don't know *what* to look for. These facts explain why, in one study, only 34 percent of browsers found it easy to choose fiction from the library's shelves. Forty-five percent felt it was "so-so," and 21 percent found it difficult.[12]

Add to these tidbits the well-known fact that a significant majority of library patrons are reluctant to ask for advice in choosing fiction. In one study, where 84 percent of browsers did not ask library staff for help, the four most common reasons why were:

1. patrons like to make up their own minds about the fiction they select;
2. staff look busy and/or unapproachable;
3. staff wouldn't know what readers would like; and

4. a question about fiction (which is unimportant) would be perceived as being frivolous and waste staff time.[13, 14]

Taken together, findings on the success rates of browsers suggest that if librarians restrict professional expertise to subjects like catalog design and reference work (services of primary benefit to the patron seeking *specific* titles), a significant number of browsers may exercise a variety of selection options that librarians may find less attractive. These patrons may choose substitute titles that will end up being less than fully satisfying; they may leave the library with empty hands,[15] or look for mental sustenance elsewhere.

We could minimize these problems by working harder at efforts to improve the management of our fiction collections and our stack facilities so the large number of people who are browsing our fiction collections can find materials they will enjoy. But we need, before we do this, to gain a better understanding of the extent to which:

1. materials meet the needs of browsers; and
2. information overload negatively affects patron decision making.

This understanding will help to improve management techniques, techniques that can enable more patrons to find those special materials that are right for them—whether they desire titles that provide action-filled plots, complex characters, or a new perspective or titles that make them laugh, envigorate their spirits, or give them comfort.

Are Public Librarians Providing Matrials to Meet the Needs and Desires of Browsers?

As noted earlier, 52 percent of the browsers in one study looked for particular (often best selling) authors without success.[16] In another study, 54 percent of those who had some difficulty browsing for titles to check out attributed the problem to the lack of desired titles on the shelves.[17]

The problem is often compounded by the fact that, in spite of what librarians perceive as long waiting lists for titles by popular authors, a majority of browsers do *not* file reserves for these titles. One study found, for example, that 78 percent had placed *no* reserves on fiction within the last six months.[18] One author concluded that, "With the length of some waiting lists for fiction, and the financial restrictions on the book fund, the majority of our readers must never find popular new books on the shelves."[19]

The situation grows even more complicated when one considers that best sellers are not the only materials in short supply on the shelves of most libraries.[20] Other works wanted but not always found include modern-day classics like *Fahrenheit 451*; older classics like *The Adventures of Huckleberry Finn*; items that have received various kinds of awards for their quality; materials by authors with long-standing reputations, such as J.R.R. Tolkien; materials in highly used genre areas, like mysteries and romances; materials featured on television or in feature films; and materials in highly popular formats, such as books on tape.

A further compounding factor is that patrons desire collection breadth as well. For example, they want their public libraries to purchase more materials and to provide larger collections of frequently changing stock to increase their selection options.[21]

To increase the likelihood of providing both depth and breadth in their collections, especially given existing financial constraints, public librarians will need to further refine those techniques that relate to development and evaluation of the fiction collection.

How Does Information Overload Affect Those Who Browse for Fiction?

Before this can be done, however, we need to gain an in-depth understanding of the environment in which the stock operates. Farmers base their understanding on their own direct knowledge and experience. But they also recognize the value of learning from related disciplines like stock management, agriculture, metereology, and veterinary science.

Librarians should try to broaden their focus as well, and work to build an album of snapshots, a series of photographs that can enrich an understanding of the complexity of browsing behavior. We glimpse a finding from the closely related field of classification theory: patrons view unpredictable arrangements of materials as crazy or stupid, becoming psychologically comfortable only when a classification scheme brings together all materials that are "about" the same thing, keeping the number of unpleasant surprises low.[22] We spot a parallel drawn by cognitive psychologists: People who browse among consumer wares of various kinds selectively filter out information they do not want, need, or understand.[23] And we scrutinize with fascination a long-known link between the searches of browsers and military reconnaisance experts: both search first at that point where they feel success is most likely to lie.[24]

All of the previous examples can shed light on a topic that librarians have begun and need to continue exploring in more depth: information overload. Information overload occurs when people are faced with too many choices. Feelings of confusion and inadequacy can result, making it difficult for some individuals to make decisions.[25] As one patron who visited a large library commented, "Using the library is a scary prospect . . . I know that nothing in here will hurt me but it all seems so vast and overpowering."[26]

Because patrons are expected to make selections from among hundreds or thousands of items, their potential for experiencing information overload is very real. Indeed, overload may be more prevalent among patrons than librarians realize, especially in medium-sized and large libraries. This is particularly true when patrons are not looking for specific documents but rather are browsing among all the materials on the regular shelves for one or two items that will somehow satisfy their often nebulously defined needs.[27] But we must remember that overload does not affect all browsers equally. This fact can be best understood if we think of browsing as a two-tier process. A patron's first action is to *browse within the stack system,* trying to narrow their search to a manageable number of titles. Only then will he or she *browse among particular titles.*

Those patrons who have had the most success in browsing within the stack system are those who are most familiar with libraries in general and with organization schemes that these agencies use. These are the people who have learned the library's arrangement; who are able to use their experience to filter out information they do not want, need, or understand; have learned to search first at that point where they feel success is most likely to lie. For example, one study showed that patrons who tended to make their selections from the general A-to-Z sequence of fiction did so because they felt they knew and would recognize many authors or had "definite ideas" about what they were browsing for.[28]

But not everyone does this naturally. Indeed, a majority of browsers (by definition) have rather nebulous ideas about what they want. For example, one study showed that 67 percent of browsers kept no formal written list of authors that they would browse for on a regular basis.[29]

Because these patrons are more prone to the effects of information overload, they have difficulty *browsing within a stack system* that is arranged alphabetically by author in a single sequence. They often prefer to make their choices from smaller subsets of the fiction collection—subsets that narrow their searches to a manageable number of titles that they can scrutinize and dip into. Only then will they feel comfortable *browsing among the individual fiction titles*—using the same selection criteria that all library users consider: factors like genre, quality, style, reading level, currency, language, format, and attractiveness of packaging.[30]

Making choices from a smaller group of fiction titles has two other benefits. It can introduce readers to new authors, while reminding them of old. And it can save their time.[31]

To increase the likelihood of enabling patrons to browse both within stacks and among individual titles, public librarians will thus need to further refine those techniques that are related to organization and management of the stacks and shelving systems that libraries now use. Both types of techniques—those for refining collection and stack management practices—are listed below.

Technique #1: Tighten Existing Weeding Practices

While older, nonused titles will not kill off our patrons the way that loco weed does cattle, removing unwanted items makes it easier for patrons to find the newer more popular items that they desire. Granted, librarians have been weeding for years. However, weeding programs have often been done sporadically, when no other tasks were demanding the librarian's attention or when the shelves had grown so crowded that no further titles could be shelved on them. The ideal practice is to weed on a regular and ongoing basis,[32] a practice that should be increasingly possible as libraries install automated circulation systems that can readily tell librarians which items have not been used recently. These items can then be hand screened to determine whether they should be discarded, retained where they are, or relocated.

Moreover, research conducted in the last decade shows that the fiction collections of many libraries can be significantly reduced without greatly decreasing the number of titles that patrons want. Roy showed this in an experimental study conducted in four small Illinois public libraries. She "weeded" 10 to 12 percent of each collection, paying particular attention to each item's past circulation. However, Roy placed the titles in remote storage, rather than discarding them, and left their catalog records in place so she could monitor the rate at which they were requested. Eight months later, no more than 1 percent of the weeded titles had been requested by patrons at any of the libraries.[33]

Librarians can also refine their weeding patterns by noting any consistent patterns of nonuse, patterns that indicate a lack of fit between the items in the collection and the library's patrons. For example, a public library in a retirement community may discover that "hard" science fiction novels are not generally popular with its patrons but that "soft" science fiction circulates well. Recording this type of objective data can help selectors make better decisions about future purchases.

Technique #2: Consciously Adopt a Societal-Marketing Orientation to Collection Management

More than a decade ago, marketing expert Philip Kotler suggested that nonprofit organizations should adopt what he called a societal-marketing orientation.[34] In library terms, selectors who adopt this approach strive to meet the immediate wants and needs of their patrons, whether these are for a novel by George Eliot or one by Sidney

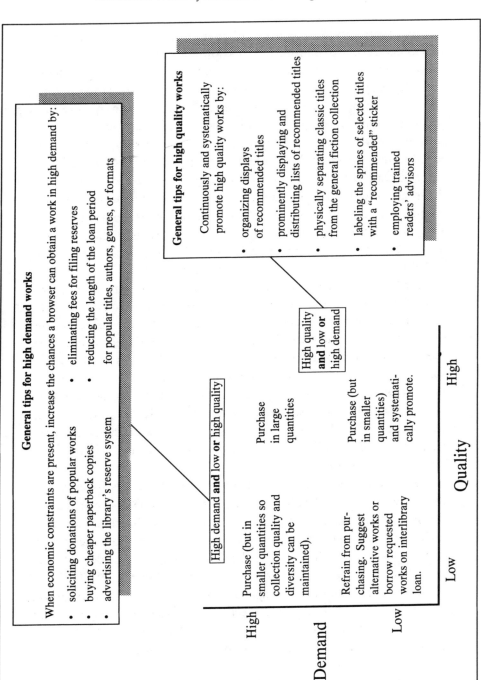

Figure 1. Relationship between quality and demand in collection development

Sheldon, while building collections that contribute to the library's roles as gatekeeper of culture and of knowledge.[35]

No research has focussed on determining the extent to which public librarians have adopted this approach. However, evidence does show that they are moving beyond a divisive discussion of quality *versus* demand and are trying to build balanced collections of fiction (and, for that matter, nonfiction). For example, a survey of Illinois public library directors showed that more than 75 percent agreed that libraries should provide books of high quality and enduring value. However, more than 75 percent also favored the demand-driven philosophy espoused in statements like "The first consideration should always be whether a book is likely to be of interest to the library's patrons" and "good service should be provided to patrons who favor best-sellers, mysteries, romances, and other popular literature."[36]

Studies like this suggest that most public librarians have recognized that "quality" and "demand" are not opposing forces on a single continuum. Rather these categories represent two intersecting continuums that measure different aspects of the same work. This recognition is a positive one, since it can enable selectors to stretch slim resources further while maintaining as much collection balance as is financially feasible. They can do this by adopting policies that advocate actions such as those shown in Figure 1,[37] actions that will theoretically allow browsers to find on our shelves the types of materials they desire (and in sufficient quantities to meet their needs) whenever they enter our doors.

But librarians could refine their existing practices by ensuring that they are *systematically* following through on as many of the actions shown in Figure 1 as possible. For example, librarians can *regularly and routinely* promote fictional works by authors that are of high quality. Librarians who have tried this have had a great deal of success. For example, serious modern fiction—dubbed "Well-Worth Reading" and promoted through displays in libraries (and in bookstores) in England—circulated twice as much as equivalent titles that were not displayed. Seventy-four percent of those who checked out materials from the Well-Worth Reading displays tried an author they had not previously read.[38]

Librarians can also refine their techniques for seeing that those fiction titles in high demand are more available for patrons. As noted in Figure 1, this can be done in a number of ways: buying (or begging) multiple copies (hardback and paperback) of titles that are highly used, advertising reserve systems, reducing fees for reserving books, and reducing the length of the loan periods for popular items and categories of items.

Technique #3: Rotate Collections Between Branches

Another strong concern of patrons is that they wanted more frequent changes of stock—a difficulty given the inability of most libraries to purchase significantly more titles given existing book budgets. But many avid readers, particularly those who use small branch libraries close to their homes, can work their way through an entire fiction collection at a rapid pace. Some patrons have solved the problem by switching branches every few years; others have simply quit using the library.

But increasing the use of rotating collections would seem to be a viable option for meeting both the needs of libraries and patrons. Use of the rotating collections has often been limited in the past due to the difficulty of indicating in the catalog when a work moved from branch to branch. But libraries do have some options. They can either leave these works uncataloged (in the same fashion that many do leased collections from vendors like McNaughton). Or they can prepackage collections so that an entire collection of items rotates together from branch to branch. For example, a large library might have fifteen different collections of books on tape that rotate on the first of every second month to a different one of fifteen different branches. Patrons at each branch can determine what titles are immediately available to them by consulting a "book" catalog that traveled with each collection. It would also be possible for a library with an automated circulation system to note that a desired title was in rotating book-on-tape collection #14, which was currently at the PQR branch.

In the past, some libraries have limited their use of rotating collections to works like videotapes, which were expensive to duplicate. But it is certainly viable to rotate any format or genre of fiction. Last year, the Norfolk, Virginia, public library bought a rotating collection of story hour books for the library's eleven neighborhood branches. The plan was well received by patrons, who felt that kids got a continually new collection of materials from which to choose. But a side benefit was the $1,800 productivity award it received from the city of Norfolk, who recognized that the plan would increase the library's ability to meet a broader range of needs while saving money for the taxpayers.[39]

Technique #4: Shifting Browsing Patterns

Physical Relocation of Titles

While librarians cannot afford to buy all needed materials, they can "expand" their collections by shifting titles. For a number of years, many public librarians have paid attention to research that shows that few patrons are willing to browse top shelves (which are too high for some to reach and present bifocal wearers with special problems) or bottom shelves (which require browsing while stooping in a less-than-desirable position).

However, librarians can also pay attention to two other research findings that are related to the principle of least effort. When all other factors are equal (e.g., when their favorite author is not housed on the second shelf from the floor), most patrons concentrate their browsing efforts on (1) shelves at eye level[40] and (2) shelf ranges that are closer to the library's door.[41]

Librarians can work with these findings in two ways. First, they can periodically (yearly?) shift the shelves so that patrons will find "new" titles at eye level. The easiest way to do this is to keep one-half of a shelving section free at the beginning and end of the fiction shelves and to shift the shelves in three-shelf increments. Titles on shelves 2–4 (formerly the eye-level shelves) would be moved down to shelves 5–7 of the same section. Titles formerly on shelves 5–7 of that range would be shifted to the eye-level shelves on the next shelf section.

Second, librarians can periodically reverse their fiction stacks so that patrons will find "new" titles nearer the door of the building. If, for example, fiction is currently arranged so that the "A" fiction is by the door of the library, it can be reversed so that "Z" fiction lies there.

It is important for us to realize that such actions are not just sleight of hand. Rather, they are techniques that will present patrons who do not browse bottom shelves, or shelves further away from the library's door, with materials that are new to them. Thus, these techniques have the potential for meeting patron demands that the library provide more different stock for their selection.[42]

Technique #5: Using Materials Displays Effectively

Patrons like and will use displays of fiction titles in any genre or format (or a mixture of genres or formats) to help them make their selection choices. One study showed, for example, that 68 percent of browsers would find displays very or fairly useful in helping them make their selection choices.[43] Other studies have shown that displays decrease information overload among patrons and can increase the circulation of titles that they contain.[44] However, displays are most effective when they are carefully designed.

The ideal display is colorful, professionally designed, and marked with a topical header that will attract our attention. Headers can be of the generic type that enables the signs to be reused later, like "Staff Favorites: Please Check Us Out," "Recommended Titles," "Titles that Other Patrons Have Enjoyed," or even "Our Favorite Green Books." Other effective headers feature types of works that patrons want but have more difficulty picking out of the general stacks: works by new novelists, prize-winning authors, or works with interesting foreign settings. Many libraries have had success with highly intriguing headers, like "Loving, Warring, Lying, Scheming, Building, Coping, Dreaming—The City in Fiction and Film."[45]

Ideally, library staff display materials on shelves or flat surfaces that are at eye level (between thirty-six and sixty inches from the floor for easy visibility). Displays that either house all materials face front or mix materials so that some are shelved spine out and others face out are the most effective.[46] Whenever possible, staff should also locate their displays in areas that are highly visible to patrons: near the library's entrance, any service desk where patrons need to wait, and (to a lesser extent) the entrance to the fiction stacks.

Libraries should also try to ensure that displays are straightened and restocked on a daily basis and change the range of materials on the display frequently (every three weeks or so) so that patrons can find something new when they come into the library.[47]

Technique #6: Fine-Tune Booklists

Libraries have also used booklists for decades—a plus when one considers that 92 percent of the patrons in one study said they would find such lists useful or fairly useful in helping them make their selections. In the same study, 82 percent said they would especially like the type of list that says: "If you like X (author's name), then you might like Y (related author's name)."

But again, librarians need to refine some of their booklist practices. Experts suggest that the ideal booklist is colorful and creatively written.[48] It should be carefully planned so the library can meet the demand it generates for the featured works: listing either the names of authors (preferably ones who have written more than one title) or listing titles for which the library has multiple copies.

And it should be distributed in such a fashion that a large number of patrons can find them. The most effective techniques for browsers appear to be to *prominently* display lists just inside the library's door (at an angle where they can be seen and picked up by entering patrons)[49] or near the entrances to the various stack or genre fiction sections. One author also found that patrons often noticed and used colorful posters, displayed in the stacks areas to brighten them up, as book lists.[50]

Technique #7: Advertising the Returned Book Shelves

One rather startling fact in a little known British study of browsing is that 46 percent of *all* titles checked out by browsers came from one small area: the returned book shelves. The author discovered that a whopping 67 percent of those who were looking for a genre title (this library did not have genre fiction subdivisions) selected their materials in this fashion. This finding supports earlier observations on overload: presumably it is far easier for a patron to search for an unmarked romance or mystery from a preselected range. The returned book shelf was also used by 45 percent of those who were just browsing for something that looked interesting.[51] Other patrons were presumably trying to increase their chances of finding a highly popular title.

These findings suggest that public libraries would do well to make these newly returned titles more accessible to patrons. For example, they could adopt the practice followed by the Iowa City Public Library, which places carts of materials awaiting reshelving out in front of the corresponding shelves for fiction, large print materials, or books on tape.

Technique #8: Use and Improve Genre Fiction Categorization

Several studies show that more than half of those seeking *fiction* are looking for works of a particular genre.[52] These patrons will select fiction by genre even when the library does nothing to aid this type of selection. One study showed, for example, that 20 percent of browsers searched for books by genre even though none of the three libraries being studied categorized their fiction. The researchers dryly noted that, "For nearly 20 percent of the books to be chosen this way does indicate some persistence on the part of readers and perhaps the need on the libraries' part to assist those readers who clearly want to select by genre."[53]

In a study that built on these findings, patrons indicated a far greater preference for genre titles that were physically separated from the general fiction sequence than they did for genre titles that were simply marked with a genre label and kept interfiled with the general fiction, since the former method significantly reduced their time for selection.[54] However, both methods significantly increased circulation of the titles so marked.

Some librarians have avoided physical separation of genre titles because they know it will decrease cross-category browsing. However, particularly in fiction collections that are very large, it would seem better to provide for cross-category browsing through displays and carefully constructed booklists given the *huge* numbers of patrons (70 percent and up in various studies) who want fiction physically separated by genre.[55]

The number and type of fiction subdivisions used by libraries of different sizes varies greatly. However, several principles can guide libraries in choosing subdivisions. These are:

1. *Use headings that reflect categories that are popular with your patrons.* A review of circulation records should reveal this.

2. *Use headings that are in fairly common usage from library to library.* One study indicated these were mystery, suspense, or spy stories; science fiction and/or fantasy; westerns; romances; short stories; historical fiction; horror; action, adventure or war stories; and classics.[56]

3. *Use headings that are easily understood by patrons.* "Mysteries" is a reasonable category. "Bildungsroman" is one that many librarians themselves cannot define.

4. *Use more subdivisions as the size of the fiction collection increases.* One study found that libraries with fewer than 2,500 fiction volumes do not need to subdivide their collections; however, patrons in libraries with 6,000 or more fiction volumes needed and wanted categorization to help them overcome the effects of information overload.[57]

One author has noted the problems associated with having very large numbers of fiction subdivisions.[58] This concern is well founded, since proliferation of too many subdivisions could confuse, rather than help, patrons. However, given strong patron preference for genre fiction subdivision, it would seem more logical to arrange such subdivisions logically within the library and label them clearly, rather than forgoing categorization and requiring patrons to browse through one large A-to-Z fiction sequence.

Also the total number of categories might be decreased by shelving together paperback and hardcover fiction titles (and videos and books on tape). This suggestion has been made by patrons, who feel that it increases their range of choices and means they have to look in fewer places for a title they might like.[59]

Technique #9: Recommending Other Methods of Browsing to Overcome Limitations of Not Knowing Where to Look

Librarians can also make up a series of attractive posters that remind browsers who are having trouble choosing an interesting title of browsing techniques that other patrons have found successful. Suggestions might include:

1. *Work your way through the alphabet.* This technique has been found to be used by some browsers.[60]
2. *Browse those areas of the library in which you have previously had success.*
3. *Looking for a book "new" to you? Try browsing the fourth shelf down!*
4. *Choose a title recommended by other readers!* The Orange (New Jersey) Free Library reports the easiest way to do this is to add spine stickers that say "Recommended by a Patron" to titles that patrons say they have enjoyed.
5. *Choose a title from our notebook of reviews.* Such a notebook might include reviews of older titles that are good but that have not circulated well, as well as more recent works.
6. *Ask our fiction specialist for advice.* The library might advertise its readers' advisory services by having a fiction specialist-in-residence available a few times a month to answer browser questions about authors and titles they might like.
7. *Use our readers' advisory tools.* A library might prominently display *Genreflecting, Fiction Catalog,* or *A Handbook of Contemporary Fiction for Public Libraries and School Libraries* on special shelves at the beginning of the fiction stacks and Consumer Guide's *Rating the Movies* and Halliwell's *Film Guide* next to the videocassette collection.
8. *Choose novels with vivid scarlet (or royal blue or lime green, etc.) covers.* This piece of advice would help librarians overcome what one author calls denial of patron access to a title's "most-often-cited attribute."[61]

Conclusion

A librarians's success in managing browsing hinges on two factors. The first is the willingness to correct past mistakes; the second is improving a browser's chances to succeed in using the library's resources. Unlike hungry animals browsing for food, those who browse the fiction collections of today's public libraries have many options. If they are faced with hardships in finding titles, they can go without the titles, borrow works from friends, or buy them—at sources ranging from garage sales to grocery stores to bookstores. And they will do so, unless librarians continue to adapt to their needs.

Notes

1. For a comprehensive overview of some of the studies on browsing, see [Deborah L. Goodall], *Browsing in Public Libraries*, Occasional Paper No. 1 (Loughborough, England: Loughborough University, Department of Library and Information Studies, 1989).

2. Surprisingly few studies explore browsing in any depth. While the studies cited here are often limited in scope and exploratory in nature, they nevertheless provide reasonable suggestions about the directions in which the profession should be moving.

3. Willard, Patricia and Viva Teece. "The Browser and the Library," *Public Library Quarterly* 4 (Spring 1983): 55–63.

4. Sear, Lyn and Barbara Jennings. *How Readers Select Fiction*, Kent County Library Research and Development Report No. 9 (Kent County, England: Kent County Council, Education Committee, 1986).

5. Goodall, Deborah L. "Use Made of an Adult Fiction Collection" (B.A. dissertation, Loughborough University, Department of Library and Information Studies, 1987), p. 60.

6. Harrison, Kim M. "Paperback Books in Public Libraries" (M.A. dissertation, Loughborough University, Department of Library and Information Studies, 1984), p. 66.

7. Public Library Association, *Public Library Data Service Statistical Report '91* (Chicago: Public Library Association, 1991), pp. 94–97.

8. Sear and Jennings (cited in Goodall, *Browsing in Public Libraries*, p. 91).

9. Sear and Jennings, (Goodall), p. 95.

10. See, for example, Constance A. Mellon, "Attitudes: The Forgotten Dimension in Library Instruction," *Library Journal* 113 (1 September 1988): 137–139; and Constance A. Mellon, "Library Anxiety: A Grounded Theory

and Its Development," *College and Research Libraries* 47 (March 1986): 160–165.

11. Sear and Jennings, *How Readers Select*, p. 27.

12. Ibid.

13. Sear and Jennings (Goodall) pp. 101–102.

14. The last three of these comments suggest that we could do more to educate the public about the kind of readers' advisory assistance a librarian can provide. But we can also also improve our own readers' advisory skills and change actions on our part that patrons perceive as being negative (like appearing busy and judgmental).

15. Sear and Jennings, *How Readers Select*, p. 15.

16. ——— (Goodall), p. 91.

17. Spenceley, Nicholas. *The Readership of Literary Fiction: A Survey of Library Users in the Sheffield Area* (M.A. dissertation, Sheffield University, Postgraduate School of Librarianship, 1980).

18. Sear and Jennings (Goodall), p. 82.

19. Goodall, *Browsing in Public Libraries*, p. 88.

20. While Sear and Jennings explored this in passing, the definitive study on this topic found that, to fully meet patron demand for 122 modern classic titles, the Montgomery County (Maryland) Library had to buy an average of sixteen copies of each title for each of eleven branch libraries. For more information see George B. Moreland, "Operation Saturation: Using Paperbacks, Branch Libraries in Maryland Conduce an Experiment to Equate Book Supply with Patron Demand," *Library Journal* 93 (15 May 1968): 1975–1979.

21. Goodall, *Browsing in Public Libraries*, p. 119.

22. James M. Donovan, "Patron Expectations about Collocation: Measuring the Difference Between the Psychologically Real and the Really Real," *Cataloging and Classification Quarterly* 13 (1991): 27.

23. James R. Bettman, *An Information Processing Theory of Consumer Choice* (Reading, MA: Addison-Wesley, 1979).

24. Philip M. Morse, "Search Theory and Browsing," *Library Quarterly* 40 (October 1970): 394.

25. Sharon L. Baker, "Overload, Browsers, and Selections," *Library and Information Science Research* 8 (October-December 1986): 316–317.

26. Mellon, "Library Anxiety," p. 10.

27. In two different studies, Baker found that many patrons experience some degree of overload when browsing among adult fiction collections that held 4,000 or fewer volumes. For more information see Sharon L. Baker, "The Display Phenomenon: An Exploration into Factors causing the Increased Circulation of Displayed Books," *Library Quarterly* 56 (July 1986): 237–257; and Sharon L. Baker, "Will Fiction Classification Schemes Increase Use?" *RQ* 27 (Spring 1988): 366–376.

28. Deborah L. Goodall, *Browsing in Public Libraries in Derbyshire* (Unpublished report using data collected by the Centre for Library and Information Management, Loughborough University, Library and Information Statistics Unit, 1988), p. 65.

29. Sear and Jennings, *How Readers Select*, p. 22.

30. For a description of how these and other factors affect selection choice, see Sharon L. Baker, *The Responsive Public Library Collection: How to Develop and Market It* (Englewood, CO: Libraries Unlimited, 1993), pp. 53-62.

31. Baker, "Will Fiction Classification Schemes Increase Use?" pp. 373-374.

32. For more information, see Stanley J. Slote, *Weeding Library Collections*, 3d. ed. (Englewood, CO: Libraries Unlimited, 1989).

33. Roy, Loriene. "An Investigation of the Use of Weeding and Displays as Methods to Increase the Stock Turnover Rate in Small Public Libraries," *Illinois Library Statistical Report*, no. 24 (August 1987): 28–69.

34. Kotler, Philip. *Marketing for Nonprofit Organizations*, 2nd ed. (Englewood Cliffs, NJ: Prentice-Hall, 1982).

35. The relationship between this marketing term and collection management were first explained in Baker, *The Responsive Public Library Collection*, pp. 18–20.

36. Hamilton, Patricia A. and Terry L. Weech. "The Development and Testing of an Instrument to Measure Attitudes Toward the Quality vs. Demand Debate in Collection Management" *Collection Management* 10 (1988): 33–34.

37. This point was first discussed in Sharon L. Baker, "Quality and Demand: The Basis for Fiction Collection Assessment," *Collection Building* 13 (1994), pp. 65–68.

38. McKearney, Miranda. "Well Worth Reading: Fiction Promotion Scheme Comes of Age," *Public Library Journal* 5 (May/June 1990): 61–70.

39. Martin, Murray S. "In the News," *Bottom Line* 6 (Summer 1992): 6.

40. David Spiller, "The Provision of Fiction for Public Libraries," (M.L.S. thesis, Loughborough University, Department of Library and Information Studies, 1979), 40.

41. See, for example, Baker, "The Display Phenomenon"; and Leon Carnovsky, personal correspondence (cited by Harriet R. Forbes, "The Geography of Reading," *ALA Bulletin* 29 (August 1935): 470–476.

42. Goodall, *Browsing in Public Libraries*, p. 119.

43. Ibid.

44. See, for example, Baker, "The Display Phenomenon."

45. This and other creative display ideas are listed in Ann Montgomery Tuggle and Dawn Hansen Heller, *Grand Schemes and Nitty-Gritty Details: Library PR That Works* (Littleton, CO: Libraries Unlimited, 1987).

46. See, for example, Sarah P. Long, "The Effect of Face-Front Display on the Circulation of Books in a Public Library," (M.A. project, University of North Carolina at Greensboro, Department of Library Science/Educational Technology, 1986), ERIC #ED278415; and Kenneth G. Sivulich, "How We Run the Queens Library Good (and Doubled Circulation in Seven Years)," *Library Journal* 114 (15 February 1989): 123–127.

47. Baker, "The Display Phenomenon," p. 255.

48. Baker, Sharon L. "Adult Services—Booklists: What We Know, What We Need to Know." *RQ* 33, no. 2 (Winter 1993): 177–180.

49. When one author used this technique to promote thirty-five fiction titles that had not been checked out in four years or more, the titles were checked out thirty-three times during the following eight week period. See Nancy B. Parrish, "The Effect of a Booklist on the Circulation of Fiction Books Which Have Not Been Borrowed from a Public Library in Four Years or Longer," (Master's project, University of North Carolina at Greensboro, Department of Library Science/Educational Technology, 1986), ERIC ED282564.

50. Goodall, *Browsing in Public Libraries*, p. 102.

51. Sear and Jennings, *How Readers Select*, p. 50.

52. Some of these studies are reviewed in Sharon L. Baker and Gay W. Shepherd, "Fiction Classification Schemes: The Principles Behind Them, and Their Success," *RQ* 27 (Winter 1987): 245–251.

53. Sear and Jennings, *How Readers Select*, p. 50.

54. Baker, "Will Fiction Classification Schemes Increase Use?" 371, 373.

55. Goodall, *Browsing in Public Libraries*, p. 57.

56. Gail Harrell, "The Classification and Organization of Adult Fiction in Large American Public Libraries," *Public Libraries* 24, no. 1 (Spring 1985): 13–14.

57. Baker, "Will Fiction Classification Schemes Increase Use?" 374–375.

58. Sheila S. Intner, "The Fiction of Access to Fiction," *Technicalities* 7 (July 1987): 12–14.

59. For example, 84 percent of the patrons that Harrison (1984) surveyed at a library that interfiled hardback and paperback books liked this arrangement. For more information see Harrison (cited in Goodall, *Browsing in Public Libraries*, p. 63).

60. See, for example, Goodall, *Browsing in Public Libraries*, p. 70.

61. Buff Hirko, "Colorizing the Library: Why Not Give Patrons the Type of Access They Most Frequently Request?" *American Libraries* 22 (January 1991): 94.

Chapter Seven:
Use of Fiction Categories in Major American Public Libraries

by Gail Harrell

$\mathcal{F}$ew would argue that the best, most thorough method for providing readers' advisory service is to conduct a readers' advisory interview with each patron. Today, however, as demand for library services increases and staffing levels are maintained or decline, additional methods must be sought to link readers with books. The Library of Congress (LC) and Dewey Decimal Classification (DDC) schemes continue to provide helpful subject access for the nonfiction reader. However, as Gregg Sapp notes in his article "The Levels of Access: Subject Approaches to Fiction," these two classification schemes do little to assist the fiction reader.[1] As early as the beginning of this century, librarians have been experimenting with methods for organizing fiction collections. In an article published in *Library Journal* in June of 1909, William Borden reported on his experiment with genre categories. Genre categories work well according to Borden because the "average library patron thinks of books by types, not by authors."[2] Newer studies, such as Annelise Pejtersen's thematic approach to classifying fiction have been conducted, but no single scheme has been universally adopted.[3] Instead, methods for arranging fiction vary widely from system to system and even from branch to branch within a system.

In 1984 an earlier survey was conducted by the author of this chapter to determine the frequency and use of genre categories.[4] A questionnaire was sent to libraries serving a population of 100,000 or more. The results of this survey are shown in the following table.

In 1993 the earlier survey was expanded to include libraries serving a population of 50,000 or more. The 1993 questionnaire also included data on Juvenile and Young Adult collections. The sampling procedure utilized in this study is described in *The Scientific Manage-*

Rank	Category	Frequency (n=46)	Percent
1	Science fiction and/or fantasy	45	98
2	Westerns	44	96
3	Detective and/or mystery and/or suspense	43	93
4	Short stories	13	28
5	Love and/or romance	9	20
6	Espionage and/or spy	7	15
6	Light romance	7	15
7	Historical and/or period	5	11
8	Biographical	4	9
9	Gothics	3	7
9	Horror and/or ghost stories	3	7
10	Adventure	2	4
10	Classics	2	4
10	Humor and/or satire	2	4
10	Detective/mystery/suspense/espionage/spy	2	4
11	American novels	1	2
11	Country and/or rural backgrounds	1	2
11	Family chronicles	1	2
11	Gothic and light romance	1	2
11	Gothic romance	1	2
11	High interest-low vocabulary	1	2
11	Librarian's choice	1	2
11	Movie and TV	1	2
11	Prizewinners	1	2
11	Psychological	1	2
11	War Stories	1	2

Table 1:   Types and Frequency of Use of Genre Categories in Public Libraries Using Genres and Serving a Population of 100,000 or more
1984 Survey

Rank	Category	Hardback	Paperback	Both	Frequency (n=81)	Percent
1	Large print	29	1	51	81	100
2	Detective and/or mystery and/or suspense	18	1	59	78	96
3	Science fiction and/or fantasy	17	1	59	77	95
4	Westerns	18	2	54	74	91
5	Love and/or romance	4	19	18	41	51
6	Short stories	20	1	11	32	40
7	High interest/low vocabulary	7	8	16	31	38
8	Biographical	9	1	16	26	32
9	Local writers	6	0	16	22	27
10	Classics	1	10	5	16	20
11	Horror and/or ghost stories	2	4	9	15	19
12	Gothic and light romance	2	7	3	12	15
13	Espionage and/or spy	0	1	5	6	7
13	Historical and/or period	4	1	1	6	7
13	African-American	1	4	1	6	7
14	Humor and/or satire	2	2	1	5	6
15	Inspirational	1	2	1	4	5
15	Latino or Hispanic	2	1	1	4	5
16	Adventure	0	3	0	3	4
16	Native American	1	1	1	3	4
17	Prize winners	2	0	0	2	2
17	Movie and/or TV	0	2	0	2	2
18	Holiday	1	0	0	1	1
18	Family chronicles	1	0	0	1	1
18	Sports	0	0	1	1	1
18	War stories	1	0	0	1	1

Table 2: Types and Frequency of Use of Genre Categories 1993 Survey

ment of Library Operations by Dougherty and Heinritz.[5] The formulas described there indicated a sample size of 215 libraries out of 1,047. One hundred and twenty-eight questionnaires were returned. Forty-two were not usable for the purposes of this study.

The results of the new survey clearly indicate that the majority of libraries are using genre categories. Out of the eighty-five responses, only four libraries (6 percent) reported using no genre categories. Included in this number is one library that interfiles fiction with nonfiction. Seventy-nine libraries (98 percent) use two or more categories. As illustrated in Table 2, the most popular categories are large print (100 percent), detective and/or mystery and/or suspense (96 percent), science fiction and/or fantasy (95 percent), and westerns (91 percent). Less popular are prize winners and movie and TV, two categories frequently used by bookstores.

For a number of libraries, format is a significant factor in determining genre classification. Love and/or romance novels, the classics and gothic and light romance novels are far more likely to be identified as a genre if the format is paperback. Conversely, detective and/or mystery and/or suspense, science fiction and/or fantasy, westerns, and short story paperbacks are generally interfiled with hardbacks or are not identified as a genre, but merely grouped together with other paperbacks.

Format also plays a role in determining how fiction collections are physically arranged. Only fourteen libraries (16 percent) completely interfile paperbacks with hardbacks. Twenty libraries (24 percent) do not interfile paperbacks with hardbacks and fifty-one (60 percent) partially interfile. An explanation was requested for libraries

Table 3: Methods for Denoting Types of Fiction		
Method	Frequency (n-71)	Percent
Combination of notation in catalog, shelves distinct from general fiction, and spine labels	49	69
Spine labels only	8	11
Combination of notation in catalog and spine labels	5	7
Combination of shelves distinct from general fiction and spine labels	5	7
Combination of notation in catalog and shelves distinct from general fiction	2	3
Shelves distinct from general fiction	2	3

Table 4:	New Book Status		
Length of time	Rank	Frequency (n=63)	Percent
Less than 3 months	5	7	11
3 months	6	3	5
3–6 months	4	8	13
6 months	1	19	30
6 months–1 year	2	11	17
1 year	3	10	16
more than a year	7	2	3
varies	7	2	3
current year	8	1	2

that partially interfile paperback and hardback collections. Frequently, if the paperback was a donation or an uncatalogued mass market book, it was not interfiled. Paperback originals, trade paperbacks, and books that are only available in paperback are often interfiled. The impact this differential has on the fiction reader looking for a particular type of book is not addressed in the survey.

Various means can be used to denote types of fiction. The three principal methods are: (a) notation in the catalog, (b) shelves distinct from general fiction, and (c) spine labels. Of the eighty-one libraries that use genres, seventy-one libraries responded to the question concerning methods for denoting fiction. Forty-nine libraries (69 percent) use a combination of all three methods. Eight libraries (11 percent) use spine labels only.

The great majority of these seventy-one libraries assign a new book status to books. Sixty-three libraries (89 percent) designate new books in some manner. Almost a third of the libraries use six months as their criteria for defining a new book but, as Table 4 illustrates, the length of time a book is labelled "new" varies greatly.

The use of genre categories is a widely accepted practice for arranging adult fiction collections. However, this is not true for juvenile and young adult collections. Of the eighty-four libraries responding to this survey, sixty-six completed the juvenile and young adult questionnaire. Sixty-four libraries (81 percent) maintain a young adult collection. Fifty-four libraries (84 percent) house their young adult collections separately. Eight libraries (13 percent) interfile the young adult books with the adult collection, and two libraries (3 percent) shelve their young adult books with the children's collection. Twenty-six libraries (41 percent) use genre categories to arrange both the young adult and juvenile collections. While only six percent of the libraries do not use genres to classify their adult fiction collections, twenty libraries (30 percent) use no genre categories for either their juvenile or young adult collections. Tables 5 and 6 illustrate the types and frequency of use of genres for these two collections.

Table 5:	Types and Frequency of Use of Genre Categories Young Adult Fiction		
Rank	Category	Frequency (n=29)	Percent
1	Science fiction and/or fantasy	26	90
2	Detective and/or mystery	24	83
3	Horror	14	48
4	Romance	12	41
5	Suspense	6	21
6	Classics	5	17
7	African-American	3	10
7	Sports	3	10
8	Historical	2	7
8	Holiday	2	7
8	Humor	2	7
8	Short stories	2	7
9	Graphic	1	3
9	High interest/low vocabulary	1	3
9	Latino or Hispanic	1	3
9	Local Writers	1	3
9	Prizewinners	1	3
9	Realistic	1	3

As shown in the tables, the two most frequently used categories for both juvenile and young adult collections are science fiction and/or fantasy and detective and/or mystery. There are, however, significant differences in the use of other genre categories. For example, prize winners is the third most widely used juvenile category but ranks ninth in young adult collections. Animal stories is used as a

Rank	Category	Frequency of use (n=43)	Percent
Table 6:	**Types and Frequency of Use of Genre Categories Juvenile Fiction**		
1	Detective and/or mystery	36	84
2	Science fiction and/or fantasy	32	74
3	Prizewinners	22	51
4	Sports	18	42
5	Ghost stories	13	30
6	Animal stories	12	28
7	Historical	10	23
8	Holiday	6	14
9	Local writers	5	12
10	Humor	4	9
11	ABC	3	7
11	Adventure	3	7
12	1 2 3	2	5
12	Dinosaurs	2	5
12	Horses	2	5
12	Romance	2	5
13	African American	1	2
13	Concept	1	2
13	Dog stories	1	2
13	Horror	1	2
13	Short stories	1	2

genre by 30 percent of the libraries but is found only in juvenile collections. Scary stories are popular in both collections but juvenile books are more likely to be labelled as ghost stories and young adult books as horror.

The use of genres in young adult collections is more consistent with genres found in adult fiction collections than juvenile collections. The seven most frequently used young adult genres appear within the ten highest ranking adult genres. One obvious exception is westerns. Ninety-one percent (91 percent) of the libraries identify their adult westerns. No library reported using westerns as genre in their young adult collections.

Table 7 illustrates the methods used by the forty-six libraries to designate genres for their juvenile and young adult fiction collections.

Table 7:	Methods for Denoting Types of Juvenile and Young Adult Fiction		
Method		Frequency (n=46)	Percent
Combination of notation in catalog, shelves distinct from general fiction, and spine labels		26	57
Spine labels only		8	17
Combination of notation in catalog and spine labels		6	13
Combination of shelves distinct from general fiction and spine labels		3	7
Shelves distinct from general fiction		2	4
Combination of notation in catalog and shelves distinct from general fiction		1	2

The survey results clearly show that public libraries serving populations of 50,000 or more are using genre categories to identify and arrange their fiction collections. Frequency and number of genre categories is substantially greater in adult fiction collections than in juvenile or young adult. Does this fact mean that genre classification is not as effective with younger readers or that it is less traditional and, therefore less popular with young adult and children's librarians? Other studies should address this important question. To denote types of genres, the majority of libraries use a combination of notation in the catalog, shelf arrangement, and spine labels. Methods for identifying genre categories may influence the degree of success of usefulness of genre classification, but the question of how the influence may operate remains unanswered.

For the library financially unable to justify conducting individual readers' advisory interviews, genre classification may be an efficient and effective method for linking readers to books. (See the experiment reported in the chapter of this book by Cannell and McCluskey for further evidence of this generalization.) For further discussion on how the use of genre categories influences the browser and impacts circulation, read Sharon Baker's article "Will Fiction Classification

Schemes Increase Use?"[6] Within one's own library, experimenting with various genre categories will provide the library staff with useful information for assisting the library's readers.

Notes

1. Sapp, Gregg. "The Levels of Access: Subject Approaches to Fiction," *RQ* 25 (Summer 1986):488–497.

2. Borden, William. "On Classifying Fiction," *Library Journal* 34 (June 1909):265.

3. Pejtersen, Annelise M. "Fiction and Library Classification," *Scandinavian Public Library Quarterly* 1 (1978):6–7.

4. Harrell, Gail. "The Classification and Organization of Adult Fiction in Large American Public Libraries," *Public Libraries* 24 (Spring 1985):13–14.

5. Dougherty, Richard M. and Fred J. Heinritz, *Scientific Management of Library Operations* (Metuchen, NJ: Scarecrow, 1982), pp. 214–218.

6. Baker, Sharon. "Will Classification Schemes Increase Use?" *RQ* 27 (Spring 1988):366–376.

Chapter Eight:
Genrefication: Fiction Classification and Increased Circulation

by Jeffrey Cannell and Eileen McCluskey

*I*magine the following, if you will: you have just been appointed manager or director of a new public library. Eagerly, you arrive on site ahead of the rest of the staff your first day on the job. You walk into the stacks to inspect your new holdings, only to discover with a shock—someone has arranged the nonfiction alphabetically by the author's last name! A quick check of the OPAC reveals that nonfiction is only accessible by author and title. Your heart starts to pound. You check your watch—one half hour until opening. You start to imagine the pathfinders, booklists, and readers' advisory services that you will quickly have to devise and implement in order to get your customers to the information they need. You vow to change things as quickly as possible, realizing the enormity of the task ahead.

Now, back to reality. This scene has probably never played in real life. As professionals, we would never allow such a thing to happen. At least not to nonfiction. But traditionally we have allowed this same difficult, labor-intensive filing/shelving method to exist, partly because as a culture, we take "stories" less seriously than "facts."

In 1992, the administration of the Cumberland County Public Library and Information Center, in Fayetteville, North Carolina, approved a plan to reconfigure the fiction section of the Cliffdale branch. In his "genrefication plan," the manager cited three influences that indicated that circulation of fiction could be increased by arranging titles in browsing order—that is, arranging them by subject or genre.

The first was his decade of bookselling experience in New York for two of the major bookstore chains where fiction was merchandised—displayed to its greatest advantage to maximize sales potential—in subject areas such as science fiction, mystery, and romance.

The second was an experiment in three public libraries in North Carolina in which spine labels and browsing sections by category significantly increased circulation.[1]

The third influence was a project he implemented as the manager of a branch of the Carnegie Library of Pittsburgh in the late 1980s, in which the entire bookstock of the branch was broken out by category, nonfiction, and related fiction side by side, as follows:

- Mystery/True Crime
- Thriller/Espionage
- Science Fiction, Fantasy, Horror/Occult, Paranormal
- Western/History of the American West
- Pennsylvania Fiction/State and Local History
- African-American Fiction/Biography, History, Civil Rights
- Romance/Relationships, True Romance

The premise was that related fiction and nonfiction subject areas shared an audience. Readers of mysteries would also be readers of true crime. This merchandising experiment led to a circulation increase of over 30 percent in one year.

The Cliffdale library's genrefication project began with the formation of a committee consisting of the branch manager, the information services supervisor, the children's department supervisor, and the library technician in charge of processing paperbacks. The purpose of the meeting was to find answers to the following questions:

1. which genres were to be highlighted;
2. what defined each genre;
3. what type of signs should be used;
4. in what order would the project be completed; and

5. how would the record of each title be changed in the Online Public Access Catalogue to reflect the shelf location of each book?

The genres selected to be highlighted in the adult fiction collection were: general fiction, short stories, mysteries, thriller/espionage, horror, fantasy, science fiction, romance, westerns, and teen fiction. The genres were chosen on the basis of the reading habits of Cliffdale's service area which to a certain degree had shaped the library's fiction collection. While no scientific study was done to determine which categories would be best received by the public, the library staff felt familiar and comfortable enough with their patrons' reading habits to make the decision. Key readers' advisory references were consulted.[2]

A working definition of each genre was developed to use as a guideline for determining where books would be placed. The definitions were as follows: "General Fiction" was anything not included in the other genres at that time, including classics, historical fiction, and gothic novels; "Short Stories" were collections of short stories, especially those shelved under the book's title, for titles not assigned to another genre. For example, the short stories of Stephen King would be shelved with his other books in horror, but *The Best Short Stories of 1987* would be shelved in short stories. "Westerns" were novels in which the setting of the old west plays a significant part in the plot. "Mysteries" included murder mysteries, police procedurals, and detective novels. "Thriller and espionage" were combined to include spy novels, international intrigue, technothrillers, and legal thrillers. The definition for the "romance" collection revolved around the question, "if the relationship is taken out, is there any story left?" While paperback romances were separated from the hardbacks mainly because of space limitations, this arrangement made it possible to organize category romances by their category. Because category romance readers usually ask for those books by the series' title instead of author, this arrangement made these books more accessible to their readers.

The "horror" section included Stephen King and his clones, H.P. Lovecraft, ghost stories, novels of "terror" and monsters. The "fantasy" collection consisted of stories of swords and sorcery, magic, and ghost stories with a beneficent, optimistic bent. The "science fiction" section bordered the fantasy section and consisted of books about outer space, time travel, future and parallel civilizations, and science-based technology. "Teen" fiction consisted of books whose plotlines and protagonists reflected the interests and attitudes of adolescents and included some titles that were also in the adult section.

A concerted effort was made to keep titles by the author together whenever possible. The genrefication committee knew this would lead to some difficult decisions. For example, while Stephen King's books are clearly horror, he did write a fantasy book entitled *Eye of the Dragon*. Should that book remain with his others in the horror section or should this title be made more accessible to fantasy readers who do not usually read Stephen King? While separating titles by one author could be confusing for browsers, it did have the potential for introducing readers to new authors and genres through such cross-over books.

The ability to change the call number in the OPAC made some of these decisions easier. If a patron is not able to find Stephen King's *Eye of the Dragon* with other books in the horror section, a quick search on the OPAC under author or title would show that title in the fantasy section. The genrefication project allowed this call number to be changed in the computer from "FICTION KING" to "FANTASY KING."

Self-adhesive spine stickers were also used to label each book within its category. The project was complete when each book was labeled and moved to its new place in the library and the call number changed in the computer to reflect its new location. The endcaps of each shelving range were labeled with signs consistent with the rest of the library's signage to further reduce confusion.

The massive task of labeling, shifting, and changing call numbers in the computer was completed with the cooperation and help of the entire staff. This cooperation came in various forms. While the branch manager and fiction librarian shifted and stickered with the help of pages and volunteers, the entire staff was instrumental in the necessary public relations and guidance to patrons who were at times disturbed and annoyed by the change. Staff were instructed to remain positive about the project in response to sometimes negative criticism and to remind patrons that the shifting was only a temporary inconvenience to make their library a better place. The staff was encouraged by the many positive responses and comments and especially by the increase in circulation.

To keep staff aware of progress, genrefication project updates were posted regularly. Verbal reports were also given at monthly staff meetings.

The work of spine labeling and moving the entire fiction collection of approximately 35,000 items was completed in April 1993. Chart 1 shows the genrefication's effect on circulation at the Cliffdale branch library (CLF) for the last seven months of 1993, compared to the Headquarters library (HQ) and two other branches of the Cumberland County Public Library and Information Center, Hope Mills (HPM) and Bordeaux (BOR), all of which shelved fiction in one alphabet with some subject spine labels. Cliffdale's fiction circulation increased an average of 36 percent, while Headquarters and Hope Mills increased an average of 10 percent each and Bordeaux increased and average of 1 percent.

This dramatic increase in circulation at Cliffdale suggests that fiction, like nonfiction, has subjects or categories or genres to which readers respond and toward which they orient themselves. When similar books are shelved together, they are more accessible to browsing, and therefore, circulation increases, because readers tend to read by category. If their favorite author has not written anything since the last time they were in the library, readers find themselves standing in front of books by dozens of authors who have similar stories to tell.

Readers' advisory software products and experimental fiction classification systems are beginning to appear on the market, which may eliminate the need for much of the labor-intensive process which constitutes effective readers' advisory service. Until all libraries can either afford the software or the labor and training costs of readers' advisory, genrefication remains a cost-effective bridge or alternative.

Let's go back for a moment to that imaginary library—since you are going to have to organize by subject and reshelve all the nonfiction so that browsers can use the collection, why not keep going and do the same with the fiction?

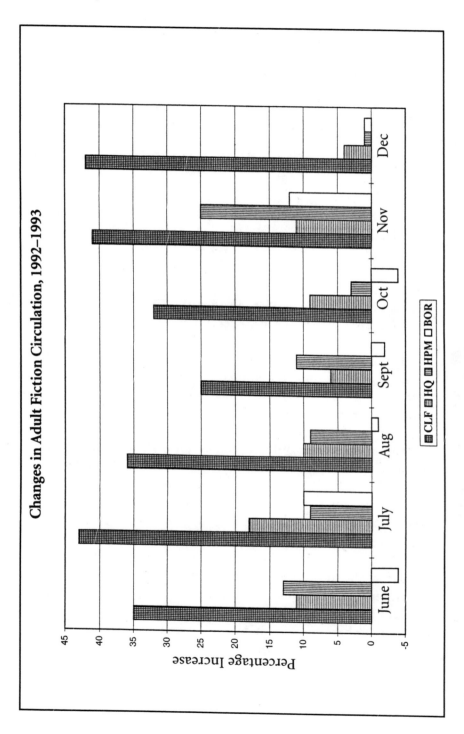

Changes in Adult Fiction Circulation, 1992–1993

Notes

1. Baker, Sharon L. "Will Fiction Classification Schemes Increase Use?" *RQ* 27 (1988): 366-376.

2. The two standard advisory tools for genre fiction used were: Barron, Neil. *What Do I Read Next: A Reader's Guide to Genre Fiction.* Detroit: Gale, 1993; and, Rosenberg, Betty. *Genreflecting: A Guide to Reading Interests in Genre Fiction.* Englewood, CO: Libraries Unlimited, 1991.

Part III:
Where Do We Go From Here?

Chapter Nine:
Reflections on the Findings
and Implications for Practice

by Kenneth Shearer

*T*hree major factors have crippled research and investigation into readers' advisory. First, there seems to be a widespread, unexamined belief that giving advice on a good book is an easily performed and self-evident activity: One reads "widely and well," and then "just makes recommendations." Our research shows that belief is completely and utterly false. The readers' advisory transaction is a multi-stage and complex task that is very difficult to do well and is very often performed marginally or inadequately. Seasoned practitioners known for their excellence in performing readers' advisory work cannot predict consistently what readers will choose to read even when presented with a good deal of input from readers (Smith). In this book we have only begun the investigative research that must be done.

The second reason that research has been so neglected in this important area of library practice is that concept analysis and classification of fiction have lagged behind parallel work in nonfiction. (Needless to say, even nonfiction has a long way to go in order to connect end users with all the material they need and only that material.) Fortunately, work on terminolgy to categorize fiction has received more attention in recent decades, and several working lists are now available. In the United States, lists of considerable utility have been developed in Hennepin County (Minnesota) Public Library, Los Angeles Public Library, and at the Library of Congress. In our judgment, none of these efforts comes up to the level of a polished, controlled system, such as Library of Congress Subject Headings for nonfiction. As we see in Dutta's bibliography (see Appendix II), while work in Denmark seems to be the most rationalized and theoretically rich in the world, it is experimental and, at the moment, impractical for everyday use. Nonetheless, fiction classification, especially the meaningful naming of genre fiction classes, is making strides both in the classification schemes used in public libraries and also—most especially—in finding tools such as *Genreflecting*.[1] Another important, positive development is the development of computer access to fiction in the form of such fiction search engines as NoveList and the Related Works features on some available OPACs. Finally, the Internet is increasingly a home to dialogue about readers' advisory, providing a community of advisors capable of providing rapid responses to inquiries about tricky problems on the job and shop talk. (See Burgin's list of Internet resources for readers' advisory in Appendix I.)

The third reason for the relative inattention to readers' advisory work is a widespread bias in America's earlier political rhetoric toward work and against play. Reading, listening, or viewing for the sheer joy of it has had a negative connotation among many decision makers, especially those committed to a thoroughly puritanical public stance. This, we believe, is an attitude that has shifted materially in American society and that, for the foreseeable future, will increasingly move away from earlier views. Indeed, we anticipate that one very urgent step for public librarians to take in order to thrive in the new information market place is to help people make better use of their highly valued leisure time. A visitor to a public library should be encouraged to express feelings about, and wishes for, constructive use of leisure time. The response should be supportive, appropriate and tend to add value to the visitor's quality of life, whether that comes through assistance in mastery of a hobby; preparation for vacations; or counseling on reading, auditing, or viewing.

Why The Current Renaissance in Attention To Readers' Advisory?

We recognize, of course, that the level of commitment that the staff in any one library system will make to this goal of assisting the public in adding to the quality of leisure time will vary. But the public librarian should examine local circulation statistics to see what proportion of that circulation is fiction, since nearly all of it is suitable for readers' advisory service. For instance, the most recently published statistics on North Carolina's public libraries are revealing: 37 percent of all book circulation comes from adult fiction and 32 percent of all book circulation comes from juvenile circulation.[2] Since over two thirds of all circulation in that state is accounted for by fiction, it is clear that customer satisfaction with service associated with fiction is an important aspect of overall service there. (Readers are encouraged to check figures at their own local libraries, where it is to be expected around half or more of circulation will be accounted for by fiction.) When we add to that fact the related observation that much of nonfiction circulation is discretionary and satisfies a need for quality use of leisure time, the case for attention to helping to advise customers on what to read next ought to be a priority of public libraries.

Furthermore, the reader should note that in the United States, the role of a Popular Materials Center is the most often prioritized role adopted; and this role, if prioritized, implies that readers' advisory services will be fully implemented. Other major roles (of the eight identified by public librarians in the role-setting process widely followed by public librarians in the United States today) imply use of readers' advisory service. The role of Door to Early Learning is the third most often prioritized one by U.S. public libraries; it is the one that emphasizes working with caretakers to prepare preschoolers for lifelong learning and a love of reading. The fourth most often prioritize role is the Informal Education Center. It implements the concept of the library as the University of the People.[3]

As the research of Cannell and McCluskey shows, an effort to make at least passive access to fiction genres through fiction classification leads to markedly increased use of popular materials. Harrell's survey of fiction classification shows, however, that the categories used in public libraries, totally unlike the nonfiction categories, are in only a few cases adopted by over half of all respondents. Baker's review of research on browsing fiction collections reinforces the conclusion of Cannell and McCluskey that public librarians can increase the use of existing genre fiction by grouping or "chunking" similar categories into browsable sections, at least in collections sized over 6,000. The investigator Nancy Parrish has demonstrated that distributing an annotated list of fiction titles that had not circulated in four years will result in their circulation.[4] Prominent placement of titles near the circulation desk or visibly at the point of entry to a library also moves books. In other words, both promotion of slow-moving fiction and classification by genre fiction increase turnover of stock. However, no one knows what mix of classes, under a stated set of conditions, would be ideal.

This convergence of trends—in the recent emergence of software fiction search engines, in Internet group proliferation, in reference tools like *Genreflecting* and its many clones, in growing numbers of meaningful works on categorization in fiction classification and in fiction subject heading lists—is changing the landscape for readers' advisory work.

Now the librarian with access to new tools and training in—or experience with—their use no longer has to attempt the nearly impossible; no longer does the librarian have to try to know tens of thousands of novels well enough to call them to mind in split-second responses to any reader with any request. The potential humiliation of not being able to successfully respond to such requests is sufficient to make many staff members shy away from such inquiries. This problem is less likely to occur when the subject of the request is nonfiction because the nonfiction classification and subject heading work is detailed and can allow the librarian using the OPAC to concentrate on the reference interview, probing for the nature of client needs.

It is now time to use the developing readers' advisory software in juxtaposition with a readers' advisory interview that poses the question of Joyce Saricks, "Tell me about a book your have really enjoyed?"[5] The librarian can follow up with dialogue about what the reader has liked about these books and what he or she is especially in the mood for on this visit. Duncan Smith indicates that Saricks's question is definitely superior to other wordings that ask about the kinds of books readers like. If time permits and the reader wishes to continue that discussion, the advisor moves over to a fiction search engine and talks about the suggested titles that come up. Of course, some readers will understand the process and enjoy proceeding on their own.

Establishing and Communicating the Philosophy of Service

The degree to which most public librarians today will attempt to direct readers to more demanding and/or better reviewed books usually depends on three factors: the philosophy of service, the reader's age, and the reader's preference. Young readers are often steered to books that are well written and well illustrated, books that are wholesome and supportive of positive self-images. That does not mean that many children's libraries do not stock series books which can seem to be trite and repetitive to most adult readers and, perhaps, to all reviewers. Indeed, such series as the Hardy Boys, Nancy Drew, or Babysitter's Club have been shown to serve important roles in the development of reading skills.[6]

But the children's librarian generally plays more of a role of educator and nurturer than the young adult librarian. And most adult services librarians accept that the readers can set their own targets and "give 'em what they want." As Baker points out in her chapter in this book, the obligation to assure that well-reviewed books are not lost sight of in collection development is reflected in a "societal-marketing" orientation, which builds collections that represent not only the currently popular titles but also the quality works that have a habit of lasting longer and being widely valued for their cultural and educational merits.

Whatever the stance of a library system, it should be thought through and recorded so new staff members may understand what they are attempting to do and current staff members can remind themselves of the readers' advisory philosophy. The authors of this book suggest that advisory service for the adult should allow them to set their own direction. That stance necessitates finding out, during the readers' advisory interview, whether the reader wants books that have received critical favor or whether they want a "good read." Careful listening to a reader's discussion of books they have enjoyed and why they enjoyed them may clarify the reader's point of view without the need of an explicit enquiry. (Since librarians are widely thought to be well read, customers may feel pressure to respond that they care about reviews if asked a direct question about their interest in reviews even when they don't value them at all.)

The purpose of readers' advisory work is to lead readers through the enormous glut of options to the ones that the readers themselves would have chosen if they knew what the advisor knows. The knowledge of which titles have received critical favor and would meet an individual's aesthetic preferences is still a very difficult call to make— it is one that requires that the advisor read reviewing media avidly because the existing fiction engines usually don't address that question clearly or directly, except by listing award winners.

The problems of offering advice on what to read next in the area of quality general fiction can be seen in the case of the reader who likes the distinguished, prize-winning novel *The Shipping News* and wants suggestions to lead to more like it. Such a reader is not normally going to be satisfied by a list of suggestions based only on the subject matter and location-based terms assigned to that book, the terms that are, in fact, used as a basis for the searches in fiction search engines. Such factors as style, characterization, richness, and inventiveness of language are all at least as likely to be important. For this reader, the latter factors are probably far more important than subject matter or location. The authors of this book believe that research suggests that the advisor should ascertain the reader's priorities in this respect during each transaction and do so in as unobtrusive a manner as possible.

After a readers' advisory service philosophy is chosen, the staff members responsible for collection development must understand it. For example, if the societal-marketing philosophy is adopted in a library system as we would recommend, both genre reading and critically acclaimed reading, as well as everything in between, needs to be acquired in a systematic manner. While not fully exploring the ramifications here, it should be sufficient to note that librarians need to decide on the implications of the philosophy in concrete terms: Harlequin series in paper? Nobel prize winners for fiction in both the original language and in translation in hardcover? The number of copies of popular titles purchased may relate inversely to the number of titles of critically acclaimed, if less popular, titles the librarians choose to afford.

Implications for Practice

We have already mentioned many implications of the research in this book and elsewhere to improve public library practice with regard to readers' advisory service. Here the implications are gathered together for emphasis and utility.

Customer Service Emphasis

One very important point in this book is that customer service needs much more attention in many libraries. The reasons that most of our surrogate clients gave for not wishing to return for more "help" had to do with feelings about the manner in which they were treated. Problems reported included perceived coolness or inattention to the requester. Often there was a failure on the advisor's part to communicate what they were doing, where they were going, and why they were using a computer. Supervisors must train all personnel to be courteous, attentive listeners—even under hectic conditions. If service cannot be provided at any particular time, the reason should be explained and an alternative provided. Library employees should understand that it is not only appropriate for a reader to ask for assistance in finding more good reading, it is a basic function that the library provides. Even fast food restaurants employing high school students are able to maintain far better customer service standards than was widely observed in both Shearer's and Bracy's research. The positive side of this finding is that customers are willing to forgive a multitude of other sins if the staff is friendly and attentive.

Genre Classification

The day of the genre novel has arrived. There was a time when the fiction side of the best seller list had few or no mystery, suspense, horror, science fiction or romance titles. That time is long gone. Mysteries by Sue Grafton, Dick Francis, or Patricia Cornwell; horror novels by Anne Rice or Stephen King; westerns by Larry McMurtry; romance by Robert James Waller; science fiction extending the Star Wars series or science-based fiction by Michael Crichton, along with fiction that is certainly not general fiction, even if the genre is not always clearly defined, by John Grisham, Sidney Sheldon, Ken Follett, and many others tend to crowd out the general fiction novels that used to dominate the fiction best seller lists.

Research clearly indicates that most public libraries that are larger than a small branch should acknowledge this trend by classifying at least the major genres that are consistently represented on the bestseller lists: Mystery, suspense, technothriller, western, romance, science fiction, fantasy, horror, legal fiction, medical fiction, etc. Unfortunately, we cannot say yet, based on research or any other defensible grounds, how many or precisely which classes of fiction are essential.

Fiction Search Engine

It seems reasonable to suggest that every public library today should experiment with fiction search engines such as NoveList and the related works feature on several OPACs. An investigator, Kim Kiiskinnen, is at the time of this writing comparing major fiction search engines in critical terms. They allow both individual customers themselves and staff working with them to find ample lists of items that may be of interest when starting from an author or title known to be a success with a reader.

Burgin, in his chapter, found that readers' advisors who read a lot of books are more likely to rely on their personal knowledge, and those who read less are more likely to rely on customers' comments or booklists. For the lighter readers, fiction search engines quickly provide titles that are related to the title that the reader has in mind; and the heavier readers will discover that the search engines can jog the memory and extend the inevitably limiting nature of one person's memory.

Unfortunately, fiction search engines often lead to some surprising and seemingly unrelated titles, but even then they may permit a more in-depth discussion of the customer's reading preferences. A problem with the search engines today is that they rarely give clear clues to the reading level or "literariness" of suggested titles. These limitations seem to afford sufficient reason to have experienced readers with eclectic reading tastes and a well-honed service orientation performing the readers' advisory function, the kind of knowledgeable staff that works in outstanding independent bookstores. However preliminary, nothing in Shearer's research showed that librarians consistently provide better readers' advisory service than nonprofessionals. But what we ought to infer from that finding is not clear since little in the professional education or the recruitment process of library and information science programs prepare for outstanding readers' advisors today. Clearly, inclusion of work on readers' advisory in the Library and Information Science curriculum is needed for students who intend to provide adult services public libraries.

Capitalizing on What the Staff Does Best

There is a very strong match between what many, possibly a majority of, public library customers want from the library and what a great many of the service employees of public libraries like to provide to customers. It is a shared love of reading (film viewing, music, and story auditing). Readers' advisory provides a structured, supported stage for the interplay of discussion about this shared pleasure. We think that a likely implication of the research in this book, especially Smith's two chapters, is that a well publicized, well supported readers' advisory service can build customer satisfaction and staff morale. Continuing education activities related to strengthening readers' advisory service have been enthusiastically received by library staffs. Baker's summary of research shows that the purpose of a large portion of visits to public libraries is success in finding congenial leisure reading. Customers need to find themselves in an environment that welcomes their searches for rewarding reading and where they are urged to talk about what they have enjoyed reading, what books they want to read next, what films to view next on videocassette, and what books on tape or musical recordings to listen to next. They have cause to appreciate activities that celebrate what they are doing and that facilitate their success.

Value Added Orientation

The staff of the public library takes by far the largest share of the operating budget, averaging about 65 percent of total expense in the United States.[7] Staff members need to add value to the library experience. By discussing with customers what they enjoy reading and why, readers' advisors can help them clarify the psychological needs that they satisfy by reading. Preference in patterns in reading—such as common geographic locations; historical settings; interpersonal relationships such as mother-daughter, brothers, etc.; coming of age; courtroom drama; moral dilemma; sexual orientation; characterization; narrative line; experimental writing; humor; and so on—can be recognized by experienced advisors working with individual readers. Those patterns can be powerfully clarifying when recognized, valuable to the customer and not unlike other kinds of counselling services performed by psychologists and others in the helping professions.

Much more work needs to be done to lay a firm base for this counselling, especially if the skill is to be widely taught and not just practiced haphazardly by those with a native gift at providing it. In the current environment of information overload, help with what to attend to from the glut becomes ever more valuable. Because human beings have only two eyes for input and one brain for throughput, the question of selection is of what to read, watch, or listen to appears to be a basic problem of the age. Readers' advisory research deals with that question.

The Diagnostics Model for Readers' Advisory

The model of the advisor/reader relationship can be viewed as similar to the doctor/patient relationship in certain respects. The reader's current, specific need, like a patient's, must be clearly identified in a diagnostic process. No assumptions or stereotyping should be allowed to cloud the clear analysis of what the reader enjoys about reading. For instance, if an African-American asks for help, merely suggesting other books by African-American authors, unless identified as being of significance, is inappropriate. Only discussion and listening skills can sort this out. No personal values about a literary canon or personal favorites of the advisor should be allowed to downplay the importance of the reader's need or skew the prescribed reading, even though personal enthusiasm can be shared.

The advisor should recognize that although the reader is a unique individual with whom he or she has become familiar, during a transaction, an unexpected need may come up. In the analogy, a patient may go to the doctor to follow a long-standing condition, for example, a cancer remission case that is being followed; or that same patient may come to the doctor about an earache. Similarly, a regular reader of Generation X writers may suddenly, perhaps because of a death in the family, be very interested in exploring father-daughter relationships in realistic autobiographies, especially if set in the midwest.

Another insight into the job can be gained by noting that often a doctor has identified the need but is very unsure whether the drug prescribed may have undesirable side effects and require a substitute. Similarly, the advisor may discover that the first suggestion needs modification because the reading level is too low or high, the genre is right but the style is wrong, the reader really is best served with large print rather than ten-point type or prefers an eighteenth-century Scottish setting rather than medieval France.

Both doctors and readers' advisors, of course, note that people change with age. For example, the client preoccupied with gobbling up science fiction at one point may move on to mysteries and/or science fact at a later time. Fortunately, both the experienced doctor and the experienced librarian find that certain needs and patterns appear frequently and, like aspirin and penicillin, certain best selling and classic books meet a remarkable number of needs. But both the modern pharmacopeia and the modern library are huge, complex collections that challenge the talents of the most competent.

It may also be that individual records ought to be kept for advisees, just as physicians and teachers consult records on their clients and students. This practice could facilitate different staff members in assisting advisees in a more coordinated way and prevent faulty memories from leading to inappropriate recommendations. Individualized lists of incoming titles could be scanned against reader profiles based on such files.

The First of Twenty Questions

Joyce Saricks and Nancy Brown are well known in the field of readers' advisory service. They suggest that an important step in a readers' advisory transaction is asking about earlier reading that an advisee has enjoyed. A major conclusion of the research in Part I, with no counter indications, is that they appear to be correct. An inquiry such as "Tell me about a book you have really enjoyed" is helpful for a successful transaction, both in terms of the advisor's success in finding readings that will be enjoyed and in the advisee's sense of feeling good about the library and the caring professionalism of the advisor. Duncan Smith shows that reader's advisors can take a written response to such a question and use it to make approriate recommendations.

If a library were to keep files on customers (with their permission, of course), surely a transcription of the response to that question would belong there. Computerized files with a record of the recommended books that were rejected or disliked and those that were read and enjoyed would not only have value for the readers' advisor, but also for the retrospective review of the customer's reading history by the customer. A potential, ancilliary use of such files would be found in collection development.

It seems that all readers' advisory work ought to begin with an inquiry into the reading liked by the advisee, but it also appears that the direction that the transaction takes from there is highly individualized and dependent on the responses of the advisee and the knowldege base of the advisor. The transaction's outcome is also limited by the amount and nature of materials available for loan at the time of the transaction. Further research may show, however, that no matter how unique and individualized these transactions are, there is one (or several) discernable pattern(s) that lead to greater success than others. If there are several generic approaches, future investigations need to be concerned with the question of what conditions suggest that one method ought to be preferred to another.

Practice Audit and Readers' Advisory

Modern professionals are keeping up with the demands of new knowledge, trends, and technology as well as honing their skills by adopting a "practice audit" stance. In order to do the best job pos-

sible, professionals assess the relevance of what they read in the literature and hear in continuing education sessions; they selectively try aspects that seem most promising on the job. They then critically
observe what works and what doesn't. They are constantly in internal
dialogue about what they have done and what the consequences are.
They regulate their behavior to reconfigure what mix works best in
their practice. This approach is very appropriate in the readers' advisory environment, where the tools, the supporting technologies, the
research findings, and the processes are all simultaneously in flux.

Where to Locate Readers' Advisory

The reader entering the library must guess where help can be found.
In Bracy's and Shearer's work, the seekers of readers' advisory usually
went to a service desk, most often a reference desk, but alternatively a
circulation station. Experience tells us that these questions can also
come at any time that staff members are working the floor. Saricks
and Brown recommend that the staff systematically approach browsers and initiate readers' advisory service. Nothing in the research in
this book identifies that one location is better than another for the location of readers' advisory.

Joan Durrance, in her work on reference questions, also notes
that customers often do not know to whom to pose their questions.
Investigators, in this book and elsewhere, have observed that clients
often cannot tell who is and who is not a librarian when seeking assistance of any sort, unlike the situation in hospitals and pharmacies.
Perhaps the most surprising finding in this regard is the apparent discovery, based on a very limited sample, that librarians do not regularly perform adult readers' advisory better than other staff members:
The range of observed performance levels was startling, some of the
best and most of the very worst coming from nonlibrarians. One reason for this finding may lie in the educational requirements for adult
services librarians as opposed to Children's Services librarians. Preparation to advise children and their caregivers on good and/or appropriate books in all categories is a typical requirement in dealing with
children's needs but is not for those planning to serve adult customers. Bracy, not surprisingly, found higher satisfaction rates with transactions dealing with children's material than Shearer did with
transactions dealing with adult material.

Conclusions

The most common reason to visit a public library is to locate discretionary reading (or viewing or auditing). Evidence shows that library collections are hard to browse and customers need help, both from the staff in the form of direct advice about what to borrow next, and in the form of indirect assistance provided by genre classification and recommended lists. Research on the subject of assisting readers to find what they want has been rare even while questions abound and the consequences are important to the field.

Public libraries will continue to be a major source of discretionary reading and nonprint materials for the foreseeable future. This is one reason, no doubt, that most public libraries priortize the role of Popular Materials Center. Readers' advisory services fit this role perfectly. Major tools to assist the advisor in the form of fiction search engines are just beginning to enter public libraries. Video stores are offering similar videocassette search engines that allow a viewer to explore film options; they will be useful in libraries as well.

Readers' advisory services also complement several other major roles that many public libraries play: as a Gateway to Learning for preschoolers, for example, and as a University of the People. The World Wide Web is also a source of application of readers' advisory service. Finding the appropriate sites on the Web that house individual interests is fundamentally the same problem in information overload that browsers of library stacks know well.

Readers' advisory can advance the cause of public librarianship. At the same time it can reward the public in search of aethestic satisfaction and a temporary reprieve from stress. Readers' advisory lends itself to study; let's make it an open book.

Notes

1. Herald, Diana T. *Genreflecting: A Guide to Reading Interests in Genre Fiction.* 4th ed. (Englewood, CO: Libraries Unlimited, 1995).
The genre classifications created for this book are well thought out and ought to be tried as a means to organize genre fiction in a large fiction collection. Records of circulation of genre fiction before and after adoption of this system of classification should be kept, keeping at the same time before

and after records in a similar community that did not adopt it. The results of the experiment would be very useful to the field.

2. North Carolina Dept. of Cultural Resources. State Library. *Public Libraries: Statistics & Directory of North Carolina.* July 1, 1993-1994. Rev. ed. (Raleigh, N.C.: North Carolina Dept. of Cultural Resources, 1994). p.15.

3. Shearer, Kenneth. "Confusing What is Most Used with What is Most Wanted: a Crisis in Public Library Priorities Today." *Public Libraries* (July/August, 1993): 193-197.

4. Parrish, Nancy. "The Effects of a Booklist on the Circulation of Fiction Books Which Have Not Been Borrowed from a Public Library in Four Years or Longer." Available from EDRS in paper and microfiche. (RIEOCT 87)

5. Saricks, Joyce G. and Nancy Brown. *Readers' Advisory Service in the Public Library.* (Chicago: American Library Association, 1989): 33.

The wording that they use is "Tell me about a book you have really enjoyed," and the wording Duncan Smith has used is almost the same, "Tell me about a book you have read and enjoyed."

6. Ross, Catherine Sheldrick. "If They Read Nancy Drew, So What?: Series Book Readers Talk Back." *Library and Information Science Research.* (Summer, 1995): pp. 201-235.

7. Wright, Lisa A. "As Public Library Circulation Falls, Spending Keeps Pace with Inflation." *American Libraries.* (Oct., 1995): 912-913.

See table under heading, "Salaries."

Appendix I:
Readers' Advisory Resources
for Adults on the Internet

by Robert Burgin

The Internet provides a variety of resources that might be helpful to librarians and others attempting to provide readers' advisory services. This guide lists three such resources: lists; World Wide Web sites; and newsgroups. The guide is meant to be selective, not comprehensive, and is limited to resources of interest to those providing readers advisory services *to adults*. (Resources specific to children are not included.) **The wise reader will remember that the Internet is a very dynamic environment and that resources are added, deleted, and modified daily. World Wide Web addresses, in particular, change at a maddening rate.**

Lists

Introduction

Lists—or listservs or interest groups or electronic discussion groups—are very similar to newsgroups in that they represent a mechanism by which groups of people can discuss a common interest. They differ from newsgroups, however, in the mechanism by which they distribute their discussions. While newsgroups require access to a news server and a news reader program, lists require only access to electronic mail.

As you might imagine, knowing that a list exists and knowing how to subscribe to it represent two hurdles to using these forums. Luckily, four Web sites exist with information on Internet lists, and an Internet list exists for announcing new lists.

A list of some 6,000 e-mail discussion groups can be searched at the following Web site: http://www.nova.edu/Inter-Links/listserv. html.

A list of "Publicly Accessible Mailing Lists" is available at http:// www.NeoSoft.com/internet/paml/.

The Directory of Scholarly E-Conferences includes almost 1,800 lists and is available at http://www.austin.unimelb.edu?au:800/1s/ acad. A list of 62 categories can be browsed or a keyword search can be done.

The "tile.net/listserv index" is a fourth Web site that lists the lists available on the Internet. It is available at http://www.tile.net/tile/ listserv/index.html, and there is an alphabetical listing by description, an alphabetical listing by name, lists by host country and sponsoring organization, a list of most popular lists (1000 or more members), and a subject search engine.

Finally, NEW-LIST exists as a forum for announcing new Internet lists. This list is the best way to keep up with new interest groups and can be joined by sending the following message to listserv@vm1. nodak.edu:
SUBSCRIBE NEW-LIST your name

1) Fiction

An electronic mailing list devoted to readers' advisory in general. Topics include genre studies, bibliographies, reading clubs, and electronic resources. To join the list, send the following message to majordomo@listserv.nsisilus.org:
SUBSCRIBE

2) Fantasy

a) FANTASY
"A forum for the discussion of the genre of fantasy fiction." Join the list by sending the following message to listproc@unicorn.acs. ttu.edu:
SUBSCRIBE FANTASY your name

3) Horror

a) HORROR

A list for those interested in horror fiction and films. Archived monthly. To join the list, send the following message to listserv@iubvm.ucs.indiana.edu:

SUBSCRIBE HORROR

4) Mystery

a) DOROTHYL

"DOROTHYL is a discussion and idea list in DIGEST form for the lovers of the mystery genre. . . . DOROTHYL is ONLY available in digest format. When you subscribe you will automatically receive the list as a daily digest." Join the list by sending the following message to listserv@kentvm.kent.edu:

SUBSCRIBE DOROTHYL your name

b) GASLIGHT

A mailing list devoted to "the literary discussion of stories written in 1919 or earlier. For the most part, the stories chosen for discussion will be about mystery, adventure and The Weird." You can subscribe by sending the following message to mailserv@mtroyal.ab.ca:

SUBSCRIBE GASLIGHT

c) MYSTERY

"The Mystery mailing list is intended to be a resource for reader-provided reviews of current and/or past mystery novels of all genres." To subscribe, send the following message to mystery-request@lunch.engr.sgi.com:

SUBSCRIBE MYSTERY

Note, however, that in order to become a new member of the list, you must first review a mystery book. Furthermore, in order to remain a member of the list, you are required to review one book per quarter.

5) Romance

a) RRA-L

"RRA-L is a discussion and idea list for readers of romance fiction. The listowners called it Romance Readers Anonymous knowing that fans of this genre sometimes have trouble admitting their preference for a good love story." To join the list, send the following message to listserv@kentvm.kent.edu:

SUBSCRIBE RRA-L

6) Science Fiction

a)   SCIENCE FICTION LOVERS

"SF-LOVERS has discussed many topics, all of them related in some way to the theme of science fiction or fantasy." Join the list by sending the following message to sf-loversrequest@rutvm1. rutgers.edu:

SUBSCRIBE SF-LOVERS

b)   SF-LIST

"A forum for the discussion of the genre of science fiction." You can join the list by sending the following message to listproc@unicorn.acs.ttu.edu:

SUBSCRIBE SF-LIST your name

World Wide Web Sites

Introduction

Web sites provide access to hypertext documents about an incredibly wide range of subjects. In addition to providing printed information, they may also contain graphics as well as links to other sites on the World Wide Web.

Again, knowing which Web sites exist and how to access them can be challenging. In general, there are two ways to find Web sites on a given topic: topical guides and Web search engines.

Topical guides to the World Wide Web are like subject bibliographies—they list Web sites and their addresses under subject headings. Three guides to try are the Whole Internet Catalog (http://nearnet.gnn.com/wic/newrescat.toc.html), Scott Yanoff's Special Internet Connections List (http://www.w3.org/hypertext/DataSources/Yanoff.html), and Stanford's Yahoo list (http://www.yahoo.com).

By contrast, Web search engines are like an OPAC—they allow keyword searches to be carried out. Two of the better Web search engines are Lycos (http://lycos.cs.cmu.edu) and WebCrawler (http://

webcrawler.com). Two other Web sites feature collections of search engines: Netscape's Collection of Search Engines (http://home.mcom.com/home/internet-search.html) and a British site that collects search engines (http://www.bbcnc.org.uk/babbage/search.html).

Finally, one Internet newsgroup (comp.infosystems. www. announce) announces new Web sites.

1)   Fantasy

(Note that many of the science fiction sites listed below include fantasy.)
a)   The Fantasy Links Page (http://www.mcs.net/~finn/fant/hotlist.html)

A very thorough collection of links to fantasy and science fiction resources on the Internet. Includes links to publishers, archives, fantasy art, mythology, books, and reviews.
b)   Fantasy Readers Corner (http://www.Quake.Net/~autopen/fantasy.html)

Covers topics from fairies, elves, and leprechauns to castles and wizards to modern day magic and parallel worlds. Includes lists of fairy books, a comprehensive fantasy book list (authors and titles), electronic versions of Beowulf and other medieval texts, and electronic versions of more modern texts, like *A Princess of Mars* and *The Wonderful Wizard of Oz*. A section for reader recommendations is under development.
c)   The Quasi Definative [sic] Fantasy Book-List (http://www.mcs.net/~finn/home.html)

Lists authors and their fantasy titles with some short synopses.
d)   The Unio-Mystica Fantasy Page (http://www.best.com/~wooldri/awooldri/fantasy.html)

Links to other fantasy resources, including some related to books.

2)   Horror

a)   Bram Stoker Award Winners, 1988–1994 (http://www.lm.com/~lmann/awards/stokers/stokers.html)

The Bram Stoker Awards are given out each year by members of the Horror Writers Association. The winners and nominees from

1988 to the present are listed here. Categories include best novel, first novel, novelette, short story, collection, and nonfiction.

3) Mystery

a)   ClueLass Home Page: A Mystery Newsletter (http://www.slip.net/ ~cluelass/)

A very nice Web site that includes a helpful subject cross-reference index to the page itself. Sections include "People" (where mystery writers tell what they're working on; includes a listing of non-electronic groups for mystery writers and mystery lovers), "Books" (including lists of recent and upcoming mysteries, reference books for mystery writers and fans, and links to booksellers, publishers, and electronic texts), "Events" (conferences, book signings and readings, rumors), "Reference" (mystery awards, the Frequently Asked Questions (FAQ) list, and links to other sites on the Internet, including the home pages of mystery authors).

b)   Crime Writers of Canada Home Page (http://www.swifty.com/ cwc/cwchome.htm)

News and information about members of the Crime Writers of Canada and their books. Plans to include a membership directory and bibliography.

c)   Edgar Allan Poe's House of Usher (http://infoweb.magi.com/ ~forrest/index.html)

Lots of information about the originator of the detective story: electronic texts, pictures, and the "Ravin' of the Week" (sometimes a poem, sometimes a bit of trivia, sometimes a comment on the page itself).

d)   The Mysterious Homepage (http://www.db.dk/dbaa/jbs/ homepage.htm)

This Danish site has links to dozens of mystery-related sites, including the "Mysterious Bytes" newsletter, mystery games on the Internet, and mystery bibliographies.

e)   Mystery Connection (http://emporium.turnpike.net/~mystery/)

An online extension of two publications: "Over my Dead Body" and "The Magnifying Glass." The former is an electronic bulletin board with reviews of mysteries, a calendar of events, and mystery news. The latter is a newsletter with information about signings, conventions, writers' conferences, awards, special events, locations of bookstores specializing in mysteries, and murder mystery dinner theater.

f) Mystery Corner (http://www.Quake.Net/~autopen/Mystery.html)

Lists of mystery writers and titles. Working on recommendations and reviews of favorite authors.

g) Nero Wolfe Home Page (http://www.fish.com/~muffy/pages/books/rex_stout/nero_wolfe.html)

With links for orchid fanciers. Now building a detailed chronology.

h) Rumpole's Home Page (http://retriever.cs.umbc.edu:80/~schott/rumpole/)

All you want to know about the "Old Bailey hack." Includes the Rumpolean FAQ, a Rumpolean glossary, tours of Old Bailey, and a link to the John Mortimer Page.

i) Sherlockian Holmepage (http://watserv1.uwaterloo.ca/~credmond/sh.html)

Contains links to all the stories in the public domain, as well as many other Holmesian sites. Links to multimedia files and odd sites of interest to Holmes fans (like "The Pipes Digest").

j) The Tangled Web (http://www.dungeon.com/~hickafric/tangled-web.html)

A new United Kingdom site with the goal of providing a variety of links to crime and mystery fiction sites. Includes authors' Web pages, book publishers' pages, electronic magazines and newsletters, and "Tools of the Trade" (links to the forensic entomology and forensic sciences Web sites and the poison information database, for example).

k) Walter Sorrells Presents Mystery Zone (http://www.mindspring.com/~walter/mystzone.html)

"The Internet's First Magazine of Mystery, Suspense and Crime Fiction." Book excerpts, book reviews, letters from readers, interviews, and links to other Internet resources.

4) Romance

a) The Regency Reader (http://www.writepage.com/regency1.htm)

Includes an explanation of the genre and a listing of forthcoming Regency titles with short synopses.

b) Romance Readers Corner (http://www.Quake.Net/~autopen/Romance.html)

Covers fantasy romances, the English Regency, Victorian romances, and frontier romances. Book lists and historical background information on the genres.

5) *Science Fiction*

Science fiction has a large following on the Internet. One topical guide (Yahoo) has 227 links to science fiction and fantasy, with 80 links to authors alone.

a) AwardWeb: Collections of Literary Award Information (http://www.lm.com/~lmann/awards/awardweb.html)

A collection of Web sites that list literary award winners. The emphasis is science fiction awards, but the owner plans to add links for other awards.

b) Beyond the Pale: Horror/Fantasy/SF Book Reviews (http://alf2.tcd.ie/~mmmchugh/reviews.html)

Reviews written by the owner of the Web page.

c) Canadian Science Fiction & Fantasy Resource Guide (http://www.magi.com/~gonzo/cansfrg.html)

Aims to be a comprehensive guide to Canadian science fiction and fantasy. Lists Canadian SF&F bookstores, conventions, fan clubs, organizations, and publications.

d) Doug's SF Reviews (http://www.astro.washington.edu/ingram/books.html)

Over 200 short reviews and over a dozen long reviews of titles in "Speculative Fiction."

e) Feminist Science Fiction, Fantasy, & Utopia (http://www.uic.edu/~lauramd/sf/femsf.html)

Features a bibliography of titles with synopses, a subject index, and a nonfiction bibliography.

f) Good Reading Guide (http://julmara.ce.chalmers.se/SF_archive/SFguide/)

Very brief opinions of selected science fiction titles "put together by a collection of Australian SF fans and participants in the rec.arts.sf* newsgroups."

g) The Internet Top 100 SF/Fantasy List (http://www.clark.net/pub/iz/Books/Top100/top100.html)

A compilation of the top 100 science fiction and fantasy books, as voted by the Internet community.

h) The Linköping Science Fiction & Fantasy Archive (http://sf.www.lysator.liu.se/sf_archive/sf_main.html)

A collection of texts from various newsgroups and other Internet sources.

Mostly bibliographies of authors and reviews of titles.

i) Post-Apocalyptic Books (http://www.reed.edu/~karl/postapoc/)

A collection of reviews of post-apocalyptic books.

j) Science Fiction Omnicon (http://www.iinet.com.au/~fanjet/sfomain.html)

An ambitious project dedicated to building a database of characters, places, and things in science fiction. Unfortunately, there is no search engine yet, although you can browse lists of characters, objects, locations, and terminology. Unfortunately, the entries are a bit hard to decipher.

k) Science Fiction Recommend-if-you-Like pages (http://metro.turnpike.net/C/chriss/)

The format is "If you liked X, then try these titles." Listed by author and title. Unfortunately, there are currently very few of either—perhaps two dozen titles.

l) Science Fiction Resource Guide (file://sflovers.rutgers.edu/pub/sf-lovers/Web/sf-resource.guide.html)

A very useful starting point for links to science fiction resources on the Internet. Links to Frequently Asked Questions, archives, authors, awards, bibliographies and lists, bookstores, fiction, publishers, and reviews.

m) The Speculative Fiction Clearing House (http://agent2.lycos.com:8001/sf-clearing-house/)

Hundreds of bibliographies by author and subject. Includes a searchable index to short science fiction. Links to science fiction authors, awards, bibliographies, bookstores, conventions, fictions, publishers, and writing.

n) The Speculative Fiction Clearing House's Page of Subject Bibliographies (http://agent2.lycos.com:8001/sf-clearinghouse/bibliographies/subject-index.html)

Everything from alternative histories to transformations.

o)   Transformation Stories List (http://www.halcyon.com/phaedrus/translist/translist.html)

A list of books and short stories whose theme is "unusual physical or mental transformation." Lists titles by authors, with brief synopses, a numerical rating, and a code that notes the nature of the transformation.

p)   The Usenet Alternate History List (http://agent2.lycos.com:8001/sf-clearing-house/bibliographies/alternate-histories/)

An annotated list of novels and stories that involve alternate histories.

Newsgroups

Introduction

Internet newsgroups represent groups of people on the Internet who are interested in particular topics. Through each newsgroup, these subscribers post news, opinions, questions, and answers to questions—all related (more or less) to the topic of the newsgroup. Postings to newsgroups are accessed by using a news reader to subscribe to a newsgroup and then read its postings. The number of newsgroups available on one's local Internet server will vary, but typically, a local Internet server will provide access to around 5,000 newsgroups (one of my local news servers has access to almost 20,000 newsgroups at last count).

How to subscribe to a given newsgroup will, of course, depend on the newsreader software that you have available.

As you might imagine, keeping up with existing and new newsgroups represents a challenge, but two newsgroups (*news.announce.newusers* and *news.groups*) regularly post lists of Internet newsgroups and new newsgroups are announced in *news.announce.newgroups*.

The newsgroups listed below are divided into three groups: general-purpose; genre-specific; and author/series-specific.

1) General-purpose newsgroups

a) rec.arts.books

The most comprehensive and general-purpose of the newsgroups. Very busy (about forty to fifty posts a day). Recent threads include "Physical Immortality in Literature," "Halloween short stories," "NPR Booklist" (a weekly posting of all titles discussed on shows on the local NPR affiliate, including All Things Considered, Morning Edition, and Fresh Air), and "short story collection recommendations?" This is probably the best newsgroup for posting what-do-I-read-next queries.

b) alt.books

Similar to rec.arts.books but quite a bit less traffic.

c) rec.arts.books.reviews

A moderated newsgroup, which means that someone is in charge of what gets posted here; presumably, this process ensures a certain level of quality in the postings. Includes reviews of fiction and nonfiction, new and old titles.

d) alt.books.reviews

Not reviews as such but people sharing their opinions on specific titles, authors, and genres. Recent examples include people listing their favorite Romance writers, calls for "your favorite book" and "the funniest book you've ever read," "looking for a suspense/mystery," and "Time Travel Books—Suggestions please."

2) Genre-specific newsgroups

a) alt.horror

Includes a regularly posted FAQ of recommended books. Quite a bit of discussion about horror films. Recent threads include "Top Ten Books" and "Great First Novels."

b) rec.arts.books.hist-fiction

Recent threads include "Flashman," "Historical Romances with Substance," and "Roman Fiction."

c) rec.arts.mystery

As the FAQ notes, the group is "dedicated to the discussion of the mystery in all of its many forms: books, movies, TV shows, films, etc."

The regularly posted FAQ file is quite good and covers many aspects of mysteries on the Net. Recent threads include: "Recent Chandler convert seeks reading," "teen mysteries," "funny mysteries," "Romance in Mysteries," and "African-American Mysteries."

d) rec.arts.sf.reviews

Reviews of books and films.

e) rec.arts.sf.written

Focuses on science fiction novels and stories, as opposed to film and television. Recent threads include stories about computer sentience, Larry Niven, physical immortality in literature, science fiction books with galactic empires, and "books that even Hollywood couldn't mess up." Some reviews.

3) *Author/series-specific newsgroups*

There are a number of newsgroups devoted to a specific author or to a specific series of books.

a) alt.books.anne-rice
b) alt.books.brian-lumley
c) alt.books.deryni
d) alt.books.isaac-asimov
e) alt.books.kurt-vonnegut
f) alt.books.phil-k-dick
g) alt.books.sf.melanie-rawn
h) alt.books.stephen-king
i) alt.books.tom-clancy
j) alt.fan.anne-rice
k) alt.fan.douglas-adams
l) alt.fan.james-bond
m) alt.fan.pern
n) alt.fan.piers-anthony
o) alt.fan.tolkien
p) alt.fan.tom-robbins
q) alt.horror.cthulhu
r) rec.arts.books.tolkein

Appendix II:
Classification of Fiction in Public Libraries: An Annotated Bibliography

By Gouri S. Dutta

Introduction

Sheila Inter, in her article "The Fiction of Access to Fiction," speculates that one of the reasons why fiction is treated differently than other disciplines in both public and academic libraries, is that fiction is considered as being unreal or nonfactual.[1] For that, fiction is thought to be not so important or worthy of serious study. However, authors like Esther Jane Carrier[2] and John Y. Cole[3] explain how the influence of the negative attitude toward fiction gradually diminished by the end of the nineteenth century. It is true that in this materialistic world we cannot survive without science, history, and facts, still we need fiction simply to satisfy our pleasure. Fiction not only gives its authors an outlet for their ideas, but also provides pleasure and beauty for its readers. It is also fact that people do use fiction for serious educational purposes.

Access to works of fiction in both academic and public libraries is inadequate. Most fiction in public libraries is usually arranged alphabetically by author's last name. Clare Beghtol points out that such an arrangement is actually classification of a kind, i.e., "classification-by-creator."[4] It is difficult to retrieve fiction books when they are arranged in such an unsystematic fashion. Fiction may well be the most misunderstood of all library materials. Certainly it is true that classifying a work of fiction according to any subject criteria is extremely difficult. Its very nature makes the task so.

Evidence shows that for more than a decade librarians like Pejtersen, Berman, Harrell, Sapp, Baker, Shepherd, and Intner have been advocating the need for greater access to fiction. Further evidence of its growing importance can be cited by pointing to the fact that now 5,500 enriched bibliographic fiction records are accessible to the OCLC member libraries through a cooperative project sponsored by Library of Congress and OCLC. The records have genre, setting, character or topic subject headings for fiction.[5]

Despite all these developments and changes in attitudes towards fiction that are reflected in research papers noted above, public libraries are still facing problems concerning classifying fiction. So far little has been done to analyze systematically the criteria that fiction readers use when selecting books. Arranging fiction works in an alphabetical order by author surely helps in placing and finding an individual work in the library. But that arrangement definitely does not offer any help to the librarian when it comes to serving the users. Their needs are usually centered around other aspects of fiction. It would be much easier for readers as well as the librarians if libraries classified fiction the same way that other disciplines are classified. After reviewing the related literature and having observed the classification of fiction in some public libraries both in the United States and abroad, this author concludes that more research needs to be done. Only a few librarians in the United States have attempted to provide some form of access to fiction works to their users beyond alphabetical arrangement by author and separation by such genre as mystery and science fiction. Further work is needed; more librarians need to get involved with this kind of research so they can provide more access to fiction.

This bibliography's purpose is to aid those who are interested in research on classifying fiction works in public libraries. In the annotations, an attempt is made not to make value judgments on such matter as writing skills, personal philosophies and other beliefs. The ultimate objective is to provide basic information about the literature. However, no claim is made that annotations will satisfy everyone's needs or that the bibliography is comprehensive. Throughout the course of this literature search, emphasis was placed on checking each citation carefully. Some of the works could not be checked because of the language barrier. However, these works are included here that appear in languages other than English with the hope that some researchers will review the original works. (LISA's abstracts were depended upon in most of these cases.) Suggestions are welcome so that if, in the future, the bibliography is revised and expanded to cover citations and books published after late 1993, librarians, students, and scholars will have a better research tool.

In summary this bibliography lists and annotates both books and articles on classification of fiction in public libraries. It includes both American and European authors' work from 1909 to 1993. The bibliography is arranged alphabetically by author. Each entry item contains the following information: the author, and if applicable, the coauthor; the title (sub title); the name of the journal, volume and issue number, and page number; information about notes, bibliographies, and indexes, if applicable; the place of publication; the publisher; the year of publication.

Annotated Bibliography

Abbey, Karen. "Science fiction and fantasy: a collection proposal." *Wilson Library Bulletin* 55, no. 8 (April 1981): 584-588.

Defends the worth of fantasy and science fiction. Discusses how they are handled in public libraries, where they are the victims of arbitrary classification criteria and may be classified either in adult or juvenile categories. Suggests that all fantasy and science fiction for adults and older children should be shelved together.

Baker, Sharon L. "Fiction classification schemes: an experiment to increase use. " *Public Libraries* 26, no. 2 (Summer 1987): 75–76.

This is the second part of a two-part series [cf. Shepherd and Baker] on fiction classification. Reports findings of an experimental study designed to seek answers to four questions that relate to fiction classification and its influence on readers. Classification does make the selection both easier and quicker. Decisions about the need for fiction classification are found to be very much dependent on the size of the library.

———— and Shepherd, Gay W. "Fiction classification schemes: the principles behind them and their success." *RQ* 27, no. 2 (Winter 1987): 245–251.

Identifies five major principles of fiction classification laid out by early theorists. Research supports the viability of these early classification schemes and later ones based on these principles. Research reveals that fiction classification makes it easier for readers to select the type of book they want. However, there is some confusion about selecting a practical method for classifying fiction. More research is needed to clarify further each of the principles discussed.

————. "Will fiction classification schemes increase use?" *RQ* 27, no. 3 (Spring 1988): 366–376

An experimental study conducted in three public libraries in North Carolina finds that browsers in large public libraries can select the type of fiction they want more easily if it is classified by genre. However, the browsers in small libraries do not need such type of classification because of the ease of scanning small collections. Two methods of classification significantly increased use of classed titles: (1) spine labeling of classed works interfiled on the regular fiction shelves and (2) physical separation of the classed works from the general fiction collection.

Beck, Helmut. "On the classification of fiction." *International Classification* 18, no. 4 (1991): 205–211. (German).

Classification of fiction in public libraries with in-depth analysis in card files and display on open shelves, or selective bibliographies, should supplement each other. Investigates thematical classification schemes used in Germany during the 1920s and since World War II. The paper concludes with principles which should be observed in the subject analysis of fiction in order to meet diverse needs of users.

Beghtol, Clare L. "Access to fiction: a problem in classification theory and practice." Part 1 and part 2. *International Classification* 16, no. 3 (1989): 134–140 and 17, no. 1 (1990): 21–27.

Beghtol remarks that the bibliographic classification theory and practice for the humanities are not yet as developed as they are in the sciences. Humanities titles classified are often by creator instead of by the more useful principle of subject. Examines the need for, and feasibility of, systems of content access for fictional works. Previous classification systems for fiction are reviewed and further investigations are suggested for finding a way which would provide easy access to fiction.

————. "The classification of fiction: the development of a system based on theoretical principles." Part 1 and part 2. Ph.D. dissertation, University of Toronto, 1991.

This researcher assumes that established processes and experimental techniques are sufficient to analyze fiction documents for the purpose of information retrieval. The thesis reviews existing fiction classification theories and systems, and uses the systems to classify a novel. The thesis then develops an exploratory theoretical framework and a prototype experimental classification system for fiction analysis containing four fiction-specific major data elements ("characters," "events," "spaces," and "times") and one general data element ("other"). It also develops a model for an experimental online fiction analysis system (EFAS) and applies EFAS to nine novels which are representative of novels containing uncertain and/or ambiguous data and to the 10 novels which had then most recently won Canadian Governor General's Literary Award for Fiction. Determines the need for further work on EFAS and some areas are suggested for future research.

Borden, William A. "On classifying fiction." *Library Journal* 34 (June 1909): 264–65.

Because of patrons' lack of familiarity with older titles and because of the nature of publicity they were exposed to, Borden felt that only new fiction was circulating well in his library. The author recognized the need for fiction subdivisions after rearranging the fiction collection into separately shelved categories and leaving the standard novels in their normal arrangement—alphabetically by author. The study found that the circulation of new books was not as great as it was under the old system. The conclusion is that readers need more guidance than simply being sent to the fiction shelves.

Burgess, L. A. "A system for the classification and evaluation of fiction." *Library World* 38(1936): 179–182.

Classification was structured hierarchically with ten main classes and they were: (0) General; (1) novel of mood; (2) novel of character; (3) love stories and erotic romances; (4) sociological and occupational novels; (5) local and historical fiction; (6) adventures stories; (7) stories of crime, detection, etc.; (8) tales of fantasy and scientific romances; (9) utopias and propagandist stories. Main classes were subdivided by nine narrower types of materials.

Guidelines on subject access to individual works of fiction, drama, etc. Chicago: American Library Association, 1990.

The book recommends the provision of four kinds of subject access: (1) form/genre; (2) access for characters or group of characters; (3) access for setting; and (4) topical access.

Haig, Frank. "The subject classification of fiction: an actual experiment." *Library World* 36(1933): 78–82.

Haig's proposal was built upon the 1899 edition of the Dewey Decimal Classification System. Adopted a nonfiction scheme for fiction. Preserved the main class designations as the primary classifying elements, but replaced the subdivision with notations reflecting genre and form.

Harrell, Gail. "The classification and organization of adult fiction in large American public libraries," *Public Libraries* 24, no.1 (Spring, 1985): 13–14.

Harrell determines the fiction classification schemes adopted by the 334 large public library systems in the United States by sampling sixty-seven large public libraries. Her motivation was to determine whether they divide adult fiction collections by genre or other categories. She found that 96 percent of the libraries physically separate adult fiction from adult nonfiction and that the majority (94 percent) separated fiction by genre. Among public libraries using genre classifications, the most popular categories were science fiction and/or fantasy (98 percent), western (96 percent), and detective and/or mystery and/or suspense (93 percent). Harrell concludes that it is time for public librarians to reevaluate the methods used to arrange and classify fiction collections.

Hayes, Susan. "Enhanced catalog access to fiction: a preliminary study," *Library Resources and Technical Services* 36, no. 4 (Oct., 1992): 441–449.

Originally prepared for a seminar on bibliographic control at the School of Library Service, Columbia University. Discusses the inadequacy of the current methods of access to works of fiction in both academic and public libraries. A reason for providing enhanced catalog access to fiction is presented; the literature on subject and genre access to fiction is reviewed. The results are compared with similar study conducted by the subject cataloging division of the Library of Congress.

Hennepin County Library. *Unreal! : Hennepin County Library Subject headings for fictional characters and places.* 2d ed. Jefferson, North Carolina: McFarland, 1992, 145 p.

Sanford Berman and his cataloging crew at Hennepin County Public Library made this book available. This is a complete list, as of January 1992, of the more than 1,500 headings used at Hennepin County Library for cataloging literary works that feature fictional characters and locales. Character names and locales are only assigned for genre subheads. Includes creator index.

Ilvoneu, Mirja, "On the library classification of fiction," *Scandinavian Public Library Quarterly* 21, no.1 (1988): 12–15.

The possibilities of the library classification of fiction are analyzed according to two aspects. One aspect is the basic question of the very meaning of classification as a method of library work. Another aspect is "What is fiction?" and "What kind of information does it give of the world?" The author discusses the schemes that are used in most of the public libraries in Finland, where collections are treated as a block organized in alphabetical order.

Intner, Sheila S., "The fiction of access to fiction," *Technicalities* 7, no. 7 (July, 1987): 12–14.

Intner asks why fiction cannot be classified the same way as other text. Speculates that one of the reasons why there is such cursory access to fiction in public and university libraries is that fiction is treated as being unreal or nonfactual. For that reason, fiction is thought to be not so important for serious study. Suggests that the classification and subject headings for adult fiction should follow the same procedures and patterns as those used for all other library materials.

Knudsen, Per; Mandoe, Ki; Moldrup, Lis Rosager. "What happened to fiction?" *Bibliotek 70* 77 (1984): 181–182. (Danish).

The authors correct the omission of Annelise Mark Pejtersen's research at the Danish Library School on online subject searching of fiction in the report of the Library Centre's Working Group on online subject searching of March '83. [cf. Pejtersen et al., "Subject Retrieval and Search Strategies"] Pejtersen's classification system was based on 296 librarian-reader's conversations actually occurring in libraries. The system has four dimensions and these are: subject, framework, author intentions, and accessibility. Using this system, 435 novels were classified and made accessible online in the Analysis and Mediation of Publications (AMP) base. Through a special course and research work in the school, the base's utility was analyzed and found to be suitable for a fiction online search system. Recommends that the book reviewer's usual statement be expanded taking into the consideration of AMP system's classification. This would benefit both libraries and readers. [Abstract appeared in LISA].

Laakso, J. and Puukko, O. "Classification of fiction by topic in the light of experiments carried out in two public libraries." *Kirjastotiede ja informatika.* 11, no. 2 (1992): 61–65. (Finnish).

A study was conducted in two public libraries in 1991 by organizing an exhibition of fiction belonging to five topic categories and by interviewing the users before and after the exhibition. Majority of 40 interviewees favored having topics like science fiction and detective stories shelved apart from the main collection of fiction arranged alphabetically by author. Also favored having the topics identified within the main collection by pasting visual symbols on the backs of the classified books. Concluded that (1) indexing of fiction in a database should be centralized, (2) book lists of various topics be made available to the patrons, and (3) topical book exhibitions be organized in public libraries. [Abstract appeared in LISA].

Olderr, Steven. *Olderr's fiction subject headings: a supplement and guide to the L.C. thesaurus.* Chicago: American Library Association, 1991. 147 p.

This thesaurus supplements and explains the LC subject headings. Contains cross references, scope notes, and, when necessary, new headings for the cataloging of fiction. Includes selected and annotated bibliography.

Ostwald, Katrin. "Thematic book display in the municipal and district library in Frankfurt on Oder." *Bibliothekar* 41, no. 6 (June 1987): 257–259. (German).

A classified fiction catalog would help readers in selection but readers appear to prefer to make their selection straight from the shelves. Discusses the practice of thematic display of parts of the fiction and popular nonfiction stock in the municipal and district library in Frankfurt. Such a practice provides an opportunity for readers to become aware of the stock that they are not looking for. This should not be regarded as avoiding any library processing tasks or as copying the West German "3-tier" system, but, rather, as providing an attractive exhibition on such themes as women in literature, national literature, humor, and biography. [Abstract appeared in LISA].

Pejtersen, Annelise Mark. "The automatic book machine in Hjortespring." *Bibliotek 70* 10 (1988): 347–350. (Danish).

This article refers to the REM project (fiction base for subject searching) of Hjortespring Library at Herlev District and discusses its objectives. Primary objectives are (1) to examine the use of online subject searching of fiction, and (2) evaluate the role of classification systems and the search behavior of readers and librarians. The databases contain information about 3,500 novels for adults and children, half of which are available in the library for users. Three thousand key words and 13 subject groups constitute the classification system, which describes not only the subject of the book, but also other characteristics of the book, such as place, time, and readability. Readers have options to generate their own search techniques based on 18 search codes. Upon identifying, readers' positive reactions to the system, a plan exists to expand the system to include critical information on poetry and drama. [Abstract appeared in LISA].

————. "'Bookhouse': an icon based database system for fiction retrieval in public libraries." *Information and Innovation.* Proceedings of the 7th Nordic Conference for Information and Documentation. Arhus University, Denmark (August 28-30 1989): 165–178.

This article describes a computer-based search system for fiction called "The Bookhouse" which is dedicated to helping users find fiction. The system was built based upon various studies including one which involved actual user-librarian negotiations. These studies helped to identify various search strategies for retrieving fiction and to construct multidimensional frameworks for classifying fiction. The Bookhouse employs icons in the monitors and is designed for casual users. Quantitative design criteria and the results of the evaluation of the system are discussed. [Abstract appeared in LISA].

————. "Design and test of a database for fiction based on an analysis of children's search behavior." *Information Technology and Information Use: Towards a Unified View of Information and Information Technology.* Copenhagen, Denmark (May 8–10, 1985).

Pejtersen discusses the issue of designing a computer-based search system for fiction for children's use based on user-librarian negotiations in library settings. Interim results originating from a research project started up in 1979 are presented. The objective is to develop and test a computer-based retrieval tool for intermediaries and children for children's novels in public libraries. Five different stages of the ABC project are outlined: (1) collection of empirical data on user-librarian interactions in library settings; (2) analysis of choice of search behavior; (3) formulation of a classification scheme based on users' needs; (4) development of an experimental online accessible database including information on children's literature; and (5) test of the ABC database. (Abstract appeared in LISA].

———— Project Head, et al. "Development and test of a bibliographic database for on-line searching of fiction for children and adults based on users' need formulation." Danmarks Biblioteksskole: Royal School of Librarianship. Copenhagen, Denmark, 1985-1986.

Pejtersen investigates how a fiction classification system based on an analysis of users' formulations of needs may work as an example for the development of a data base providing combination-mode search facilities to library users. Attempts to isolate the influence of a computer-based tool on users' fiction searching behavior as well as on the librarian/user interaction. Illuminate the way in which an online retrieval system can serve irrespective of the social status of the users. A group of 50 children and adults will be asked to use the database to evaluate the performance characteristic of the database developed. [Abstract appeared in LISA].

———— "Fiction and library classification." *Scandinavian Public Library Quarterly* 11, no. 1 (1978.): 5–12

Author-based alphabetical arrangement of fiction classification in public libraries is found not to be helpful to the librarian serving the public. Experiments with alternative schemes result in no permanent success. Failures of these experiments are due to the fact that they: (1) confused arrangement systems with search systems; (2) unsuccessfully attempted to apply formal classification structures; and (3) chose genre-classification with the assumption that they are identical to users' needs and are sufficiently descriptive. The problem can only be solved by a classification system which can serve several aspects of the users' needs. Based on analysis of 160 actual user-librarian conversations about fiction recorded under everyday library conditions in Danish public libraries in 1973 to 1974 and a further analysis of 134 conversations recorded in 1976, it was found that a classification must include certain aspects: (1) subject matter; (2) type of frame; (3) author's intentions; and (4) accessibility. Based on this scheme a card catalog has been established for the staff in public library at Roskilde, Denmark.

————, and Austin Jutta. "Fiction retrieval: experimental design and evaluation of a search system based on users' value criteria." Part 1 and part 2. *Journal of Documentation,* 39, no. 4 (December 1983): 230–246; 40, no.1 (March 1984): 25–35.

This two-part articles deals with the development and evaluation of a classification system for fiction based on an analysis of users' formulations of needs. Fiction readers' criteria for book selection are identified and are related to several features, such as subject matter, emotional experience, readability, etc. Traditional classification systems for fiction and attempts to introduce alternative systems are reviewed and their inadequacies are discussed. New retrieval tools have been constructed on the basis of a multidimensional classification system. These tools, such as a systematic catalog and alphabetic indexes, are tested in actual laboratory conditions in a number of search tests. Suggestions are made for further tests in future.

———— "Investigation of search strategies in fiction based on an analysis of 134 user-librarian conversations." Papers presented at the International research forum on information science (3rd, Oslo, Norway, 1979).

In this research, based on an analysis of 134 actual user-librarian conversations on fiction conducted in Danish public libraries in 1976, four search patterns were identified. These are: (1) a bibliographical search strategy with instrumental assistance which involve little or no help from the librarian; (2) bibliographical strategy with verification assistance; (3) an analytical strategy which is a quantitative approach for suggesting a selection; and (4) an empirical strategy by which the librarian recommends a selection based on his empirical classification of the user. Describes the need for a tool providing the librarian with book contents structured according to users' needs. [Abstract appeared in LISA].

———— Project Head; Austin, J.; Andersen, H.; Mogens, J., "Subject retrieval and search strategies in the searching of fictive literature." Danmarks Biblioteksskole: Royal School of Librarianship. Copenhagen, Denmark, 1978–1983.

This work discusses the designs and tests of the effectiveness of new manual and online search tools based on the classification scheme developed by the author. Also evaluates the search characteristics of the users when they handle the new tools to extract their information. Controlled experiments are conducted using two manual tools which are: a systematic card catalog and an alphabetical subject index. The object of the experiment is to measure the effectiveness of these search tools in answering questions usually encountered in public libraries. Based on the same classification scheme for fiction, a catalog was designed combining the principles underlying the systematic card catalog and the alphabetical subject index. The entries displayed by the three manuals were put into a database which facilitated searches by different groups of searchers. [Abstract appeared in LISA].

Rutzen, Ruth. "Shelving for readers." *Library Journal* 77, no. 6 (March 1952): 478-482.

In 1941, an experiment was undertaken at Detroit Public Library by which books, both fiction and nonfiction, were arranged by reader interest rather than strictly by subject content. The experiment was supported by a special allotment which provided an opportunity to put a collection of about three thousand books under 9 primary categories. The response to this arrangement from the public was immediate and favorable. Within a few years it became evident that the Dewey arrangement on the bookmobile was not helpful, and an informal grouping was introduced for the bookmobile. Eventually, the same experiment was repeated in branch libraries, including the newly established ones. The branch librarians involved in the experiment found that approximately twelve main categories could reflect the individual's dominant interests. This endeavor helped to develop better knowledge of the content of the book, improved book selection and did not hinder reference work.

Sapp, Gregg. "The levels of access: subject approaches to fiction." *RQ* 25, no. 4 (Summer 1986): 488–497.

That complexity and a lack of uniformity in fiction classification are due to its special nature has been recognized. This paper reviews various classification schemes that are being used and evaluates their effectiveness from the perspective of their usefulness in readers' fiction selection. The levels of concept access that furnish the common point of reference in all comparisons have two facets: the level of detail at which subject is conveyed, and the number of access points that are provided. None of the conventional classification systems, such as DDC and LC, are found to be helpful to a browser. Subject headings for card catalogs and print indexes are found to enhance the topical access. Experiments in online fiction cataloging, which provide the means to retrieve a fictional work according to several subject components, are discussed. Greater subject access to fiction would be popular with library patrons. However, the precise nature of access to fiction needs to be studied systematically.

Shepherd, Gay W., Baker, Sharon L. "Fiction classification: a brief review of the research." *Public Libraries* 26, no. 1 (Spring 1987): 31–32.

This is the first part of a two-part series [cf. Baker, "Fiction Classification Schemes"] on fiction classification. A survey of literature regarding fiction classification in public libraries finds substantial evidence which shows that classifying fiction by genre helps patrons in finding the type of book they want. Identifies questions that are yet to be answered. One such question is "how many categories of genre subdivision should libraries use?"

Soldner, Dean. "Help your patrons find the fiction they want." *Unabashed Librarian* 81(1991): 28–32.

Soldner discusses the way librarians can provide help to patrons in fiction selection. Suggests the creation of a "fiction-finder" database using reviews which usually provide enough information to characterize fictions. The database serves many purposes which include (A) the provision of bibliographies for patrons, (B) help in preparing topical displays, and (C) help in reference related questions. Justifies contention that a fiction-finder database is a relatively inexpensive method to serve the users in their fiction selection.

Spiller, David. "The provision of fiction for public library," *Journal of Librarianship* 12 (Oct. 1980): 238–65.

A survey was conducted to determine what types of fiction are issued in public libraries, how novels are selected by the readers, and also their reading habits. Also recorded users' observations on other matters such as preferences in physical format, fiction buying and library booklists. The survey questionnaire was administered to a total of 500 readers in four British public libraries. The ultimate objective of the study was to provide information of practical importance so that librarians could use it for selection—as well as promotion—of fiction in public libraries.

Teresinska, Ann. "Systems of arrangement and notation of fiction for children and young people in Polish libraries: a proposal for a universal system." *Poradnik Bibliotekarza* 4 (1988): 15–18. (Polish).

In school libraries in Poland children's fiction classification is based on a division by type of fiction, with no division by level of difficulty, while that in public libraries combines a notation for both (type of fiction and level of difficulty). Proposes a unified system which divides fiction by level of difficulty. Further suggests books to arrange alphabetically by authors and then subdivide by category type. Categories can be distinguished by color bands on spine. [Abstract appeared in LISA].

Walker, R. S. "Problem child: some observations on fiction, with a sketch of a new system of classification." *The Librarian and the Book World* 47(1958): 21–28.

Walker used Ranganathan's classification method. A definition of the novel was related to and expanded with Ranganathan's five fundamental concepts of facet analysis resulting in four divisions: (1) literature: language and period; (2) narrative: form, plot, style; (3) subject: period, geographical, theme objective, etc.; (4) author: bibliographical information. This hierarchical classification scheme contains about 250 classes, implying very complex symbols for book description.

Walker, Robert. "Categorization," *SLA News* 174 (Mar-Apr. 1983): 17.

Comments are made on mismatch between the common forms of stock presentation and the observed patterns of public library use. Fiction needs categorization, or at least, some standard description of the contents of novels, meaning that librarians must analyze books and relate them to readers.

Acknowledgments

Out of many excellent sources, few deserve my special recognition. These are *Library Literature;* LISA database; and ERIC database. Special thanks goes to Susan Hayes and Clare Beghtol for using their research work as a reference source. I could not have completed this bibliography without the diligent, thoughtful, and kind assistance of Dr. Kenneth Shearer, professor of the School of Library and Information Sciences at North Carolina Central University.

Notes

1. Inter, Sheila. "The Fiction of Access to Fiction," *Technicalities* 7, no. 7 (July 1987): 12–14.

2. Carrier, Esther Jane. *Fiction in Public Libraries: 1900-1950* (Littleton, CO: Libraries Unlimited, 1985).

3. Cole, John Y. "Storehouse and Workshops: American Libraries and the Uses of Knowledge," in *The Organization of Knowledge of Modern America, 1860-1920,* ed. Alexandra Oleson and John Voss (Baltimore: Johns Hopkins University Press, 1979), p. 368.

4. Beghtol, Clare. "Access to Fiction: A problem in classification theory and practice. Part 1," *International Classification* 16, no. 3 (1989): 136.

5. Chelton, Mary K. "Read Any Good Books Lately?" *Library Journal* 118 (May 1993):36–37.

Index

About the Contributors

Sharon (Shay) L. Baker is an associate professor at the School of Library and Information Science at the University of Iowa. Her B.S.Ed. was earned at Ohio State University; her M.L.S. at Kent State University; and her Ph.D. at the University of Illinois. She is the author of "The Responsive Public Library Collection: How to Develop and Market It" and "The Measurement and Evaluation of Library Services." She is the editor of "Adult Services" in *RQ* and a frequent contributor to the professional literature. Her interests are in public librarianship, marketing, reading guidance, and management.

Pauletta Brown Bracy is an associate professor at the School of Library and Information Sciences at North Carolina Central University. She received her M.L.S. from the University of Pittsburgh and her Ph.D. from the University of Michigan. She specializes in teaching about materials and services for children and young adults. An active member of A.A.S.L., she has contributed to the "School Library Media Annual" for many years. Her research interests include ethnic materials for children, readers' advisory services, and intellectual freedom.

Robert Burgin is an associate professor at the School of Library and Information Sciences at North Carolina Central University. He earned his bachelor's degree from Duke University, and both his M.L.S. and Ph.D. degrees from the University of North Carolina-Chapel Hill. He has served as associate director at Forsyth County Public Library (Winston-Salem, N. C.), and he also served as editor of "North Carolina Libraries" from 1983 to 1985. He has co-edited the book "Library Overdues: Analysis, Strategies and Solutions to the Problem," and he is widely published, a consultant on library automation, and offers workshops on the Internet.

Jeffrey Cannell is director at the Wayne County Public Library in Goldsboro, N.C. His M.L.S. comes from the University of New York, Albany. Earlier he served in several posts at the Carnegie Library of Pittsburgh. He is active in both the North Carolina Library Association and the North Carolina Public Library Directors Association.

Gouri S. Dutta is catalog librarian at the Shepard Memorial Library at North Carolina Central University. She received her B.A. degree from Calcutta University, India, and her B.Ed. degree from Gauhati. Her M.L.S. degree is from North Carolina Central University. She has been involved in cataloging and bibliographic work and she is proficient in several languages.

Frank Exner, Little Bear, is a Squamish Indian and is employed as an information specialist at Northern Telecom. His undergraduate degree is from Bowling Green State University. He is completing his master's degree in information science at North Carolina Central University. His plans include pursuing a Ph.D. in library and information sciences and helping to meet the information needs of American Indians.

E. Gail Harrell serves as systems administrator for all libraries in Southeastern Wake County, North Carolina. Her B.A. is from North Carolina State University and her M.L.S. was earned at North Carolina Central University. She has published a survey of fiction genres used in public libraries in "Public Libraries" and has spoken at conferences, institutes, and seminars.

Eileen McCluskey is head of reference services at the Jefferson County Public Library Evergreen Branch in Evergreen, Colorado. Her M.L.S. is from Rutgers University School of Communication, Information and Library Studies. She also has professional experience in Pennsylvania and North Carolina.

Kenneth Shearer is a professor at the School of Library and Information Sciences at North Carolina Central University. His A.B. is from Amherst College and his M.L.S. and Ph.D. degrees were earned at Rutgers University. From 1978 to 1988 he served as Editor of "Public Libraries." He co-edited "Politics and the Support of Libraries," and has more than thirty publications to his credit, most of which deal with either public librarianship or the geography of information. His library practice was in Peninsula Public Library (New York) and Detroit Public Library. His teaching areas include public libraries and research methods.

Duncan Smith is product manager for NoveList, CARL Corp.'s electronic readers' advisory resource. His B.A. and M.L.S. degrees were earned at the University of North Carolina, Chapel Hill. He is a nationally known trainer in readers' advisory services. He has served as Continuing Education Coordinator at North Carolina Central University and worked in public libraries in North Carolina and Georgia. Most of his publications deal with continuing education for librarians.

Other Titles of Interest in the
Neal-Schuman NetGuide Series